I0146922

UNEXPLORED INTERIOR

Jay O Sanders

BROADWAY PLAY PUBLISHING INC
224 E 62nd St, NY, NY 10065
www.broadwayplaypub.com
info@broadwayplaypub.com

UNEXPLORED INTERIOR
© Copyright 2014 by Jay O Sanders

First printing: December 2014
Second printing: February 2015
I S B N: 978-0-88145-614-1

Book design: Marie Donovan
Page make-up: Adobe InDesign
Typeface: Palatino
Printed and bound in the U S A

PREFACE

UNEXPLORED INTERIOR is a play written by the
extraordinary actor, Jay O Sanders. It was crafted out
of mountainous research, numerous interviews, long
travel, and the passion of a great big heart. It is a story
about why it is necessary to tell stories; not just because
stories entertain us, or even teach us interesting new
things; but because stories keep worlds alive; worlds
that, without stories (and art and theater), will be
forever lost. In this way, stories, as articulated in
UNEXPLORED INTERIOR, are important in and of
themselves.

The story told in Jay's play is one of unimaginable
horror. And it is told to us through numerous different
points of view; from those who believed themselves
to be only observers or a witness, to participants in
the evil itself. However, this story never attempts to
explain away how an evil, such as that which occurred
in Rwanda in 1994, could occur, rather, the purpose of
the play, it seems to me, is to give voice to impotent
cries, expression of rage and confusion and loss. That
is, to give voice to, what one wily character in the
play, the iconic Mark Twain, calls— "The god-damned
human race".

Damned. That is how the characters of this play come
across; damned by ignorance and tribal hatreds, and
by a world that would just as soon forget or look away
or close its eyes. Felicien, the beautifully rendered aged

Tutsi storyteller, whose murder, for me, is the most
wrenching of the play, describes his world this way, in,
of course, a story or fable:

"Once there was a monster who swallowed everything.
Every day, villagers brought food to him, huge
quantities of food, though he was never satisfied. In
desperation, they gathered together all the resources
of the world and gave those to him. He ate them, as
well.... He devoured the earth, the sun, the moon, the
stars but was still hungry. Then, as nothing remained,
neither in the heavens nor on the earth, he looked at his
hand. He thought it huge, plump and appetizing. ... In
the end—he consumed himself altogether."

We, human beings, —and I think Jay really means
we—sit on an abyss, with the potential to consume our
own selves.

Genocide is an impossible subject for art. Many have
said this. And Jay certainly knows this; in the play,
the wise old Tutsi story-teller addresses this quandary
head on. He speaks to us, though now we know he is
dead, murdered by a young boy, who earlier we had
gotten to know as an innocent boy playing ball. "It is
important to remember," Felicien tell us, and this ends
the play, "that it was not 800,000 or a million people
that were killed. It was one person. Then another. Then
another." Each one "a story" he then explains to us;
thus implying, each a story, that must be kept alive.

I first met Jay over thirty years ago, when he acted in
a one-act play of mine at Arena Stage in Washington.
We have been friends ever since; and more recently,
along with his equally brilliant actress-wife, Maryann
Plunkett, he's been a partner in a series of plays
of mine, THE APPLE FAMILY plays, at the Public
Theater. It was while rehearsing these plays that Jay
first asked me to read UNEXPLORED INTERIOR.

Right away I saw its ambition, both in scale and
complexity; here was a rare play of real size, where
politics, horrific real events, literary reference all
swirled together in the same pot. Mark Twain tells us
his story; the young Tutsi filmmaker tries to record
his for us; the black American teacher discovers hers;
the Canadian Peacekeeping General confronts his
and maybe ours. A complex expression of profoundly
complex and unimaginable events; from that very
first reading I found in UNEXPLORED INTERIOR
a passionate, heart-felt, crie de coeur, pleading its
case for us all to find our humanity in the face of the
unimaginably inhuman.

Richard Nelson

On May 11, 2014, (Mother's Day) in the middle of
the 20-year commemoration of the 1994 Genocide
in Rwanda, an historic event took place. Using the
latest computer technology and with the assistance
of a dedicated team at Google, a two-way online
transmission—a Google+ Hangout on Air—linked the
theater of the Museum of Jewish Heritage in New York
City's Battery Park with the new outdoor amphitheater
of the Kigali Memorial Center in Rwanda. For four
full hours these two communities came together to
communicate and experience a concert reading by
professional actors of UNEXPLORED INTERIOR.
Groups also logged in to watch from ten other
countries around the world.

The audience in New York included officers of the
United Nations, members of the New York theater
community, friends, family of all ages, and genocide
survivors from Rwanda, Sudan, Kosovo, Armenia
and Germany. In Kigali, genocide survivors were
joined by families and students, all sitting within 100
feet of a mass grave of over 250,000 bodies. Before the
reading began, both groups were introduced and gave
welcoming messages.

At the end, reactions were shared, followed by a
candle-lighting ceremony which in New York included
a Holocaust survivor in her 80s, a genocide survivor
in her 40s, and the playwright's 20 year-old son, while
the audience joined by lighting up their cell phones.
Outdoors in Kigali, the entire audience lit candles.

left to right: Glenna Grant, Craig Alan Edward, Sharon Washington, Marlyne Barrett, Arthur French, Owiso Odera, Nile Bullock, Jamie Sanders, Jay O Sanders, Fritz Weaver, Luna Kaufman, James Smith, Michael McKean

photo by Joe Goldman

The May 11, 2014 NY/Kigali Google+ Hangout on Air concert reading of UNEXPLORED INTERIOR was produced by Daniel Neiden with the following cast and creative contributors:

FELICIEN .... Arthur French
RAYMOND... Owiso Odera
ALPHONSE...Irungu Mutu
BOY ....Nile Bullock
ALAN/GENERAL ROMEO DALLAIRE .... Michael McKean
KATE ....Sharon Washington
THOMAS SIBOMANA ....Charles Parnell
CATHERINE BUNYANYEZI..........................Marlyne Barrett
D J/PRESIDENTIAL GUARD/
MAN AT DOOR................................. Craig Alan Edwards
MARK TWAIN..Fritz Weaver
R P F SOLDIER/DOMINIQUE/
MELVIN PHILLIPS ....Matthew Murumba
COLONEL THEONESTE BAGASORA......... James A Williams
INNOCENT... Clark Jackson
BELLMAN LARRY/FRENCH OFFICIAL/
FRENCH PILOT/BELGIAN PEACEKEEPER/
FLIGHT ATTENDANT LARRY....................... Benjamin Thys

Stage Directions..Glenna Grant

Director..James Glossman
Sound Design...Jeff Knapp
Projection Design ....Joan Grossman
Sound Engineer & Projection Operator .... Liz Blessing
Production Stage Manager.................Katharine Fergerson
Assistant Stage Managers . Rose Riccardi, Luke Anderson

Associate Producer......... Carol Ostrow & the Flea Theater
Google+ HoA Producer ....Paula Gil Rodriguez
Livestream Producer/Director .... Kathryn Velvel Jones &
Virtual Arts TV
N Y Hosts .... Nick Lopez & Eugenie Mukeshimana
Kigali Hosts ....Hope Azeda & Freddy Mutanguha

N Y Support Team: Emmanuel Ruranga, MS.LPC, Erika
Feldman, Luna Kaufman, Jennifer Brunetti, Andy
Hamingson, Frankie Faison, Paul Murphy, Rachel
Murphy, the Genocide Survivors Support Network,
the Brotherhood Synagogue, and Mandy Hackett & the
Public Theater

Kigali Support Team: Raymond Kalisa, Pierre Kayitana,
Peace Rwivanga, Maurice Kagame, Simon Iarwema,
James Smith, David Brown & the AEGIS Trust, Yves
Kamuronsi, Honore Gatera, Mona Friedrich, Andrew
Fearn

CHARACTERS

FELICIEN, *old Tutsi storyteller*
RAYMOND, *his Tutsi grandson, a young filmmaker*
ALPHONSE, RAYMOND'*s best friend, Hutu*
BOY, *Rwandan*
CAT-REEN BUNYANYEZI, *Tutsi woman, mid-30s*
HOTEL BELLMAN/LARRY, *white American*
GENERAL ROMEO DALLAIRE, *Canadian peacekeeping CMDR, white, 50s*
MARK TWAIN, *the great white American writer, 70s or 80s*
ALAN, *white American filmmaker and N Y U professor, 50s*
KATE, *black American film editor*
THOMAS SIBOMANA, *Hutu historian and government minister, 40s*
D J, *black disc jockey at R T L M, extremist Hutu radio station*
COLONEL BAGASORA, *Hutu architect of the genocide, 50s*
FRENCH OFFICIAL, *white*
PRESIDENTIAL GUARD, *elite Hutu government soldier, 30s*
INNOCENT, *Hutu refugee from Burundi, 20s or 30s*
R P F SOLDIER, *invading Tutsi rebel army*
FRENCH PILOT, *white pilot of Habyarimana's private jet*
DOMINIQUE, *employee at the French Embassy*
BELGIAN UNAMIR, *white soldier*
FLIGHT ATTENDANT, *white male*
MELVIN PHILLIPS, *American businessman*

There are various opportunities for doubling.

AUTHOR'S NOTE

Although the play's imagery is, at times, epic, any of it can be easily achieved in the most modest of theatrical ways. It is a play about storytellers and as such, should invite the audience's imagination. A bare stage and open heart will be our best friends in this journey.

For Jamie Sanders

And in deepest gratitude for the collaboration and support of

James Glossman and Maryann Plunkett

Conscience is a dog that does not stop us from passing but that we cannot prevent from barking.

Nicolas de Chamfort, writer (1741-1794)

ACT ONE

(Morning. FELICIEN *sits on a hillside.)*

FELICIEN: When the sun breaks across this hill, the world lifts its head and opens its eyes. The smell of charcoal fires tickles the nose, as every family starts its day. Somewhere, a dog barks, a human voice echoes, a goat bleats and the bells that hang around the necks of our beloved long-horn cows call out for our attention. A baby cries, another answers; from house to house, from hill to hill. A truck in the distance honks out a warning as it presses its way to market. The morning mist still sleeps in the valleys, cushioning the hillsides and kissing the fields.

Two little boys go by, holding hands and laughing. One carries a fishing line, the other a panga; a machete, for clearing the brush. The tall grass sparkles as the sun hits the dewdrops, making a field of diamonds. This is Rwanda, the beginning and end of the earth. She is beautiful beyond words. Imana smiles on her thousand pregnant hills. I feel sad for anyone who does not know the joy of waking up on this hillside, receiving the blessings of a new day, here at the center of the universe.

(A surge of East African drums. A young Intore DANCER *leaps onto the stage, stomping his feet and jumping into the air.)*

FELICIEN: I used to be able to jump that high. But
time has married me to the earth and taught me to be
humble. That's my grandson, Raymond. He is a good
boy. When I was his age, I had the great honor to dance
at the court of the Mwami—Mutara Rudahigwa, the
last great Tutsi king of Rwanda. The dance of Tutsi
pride we call "Intore". "The Chosen Ones." We were
known as the fiercest warriors in the world. And, of
course, we like to say we are the best dancers, also. My
friend, Emmanuel, when I have tripped, will always
ask, "Felicien, what dance is this?" And then, I lose my
feet completely and fall down laughing.

(RAYMOND *changes out of his headdress, skirt, and ankle
bracelets into jeans, running shoes, and a Michael Jordan
T-shirt.*)

FELICIEN: For as long as has been told, Our ancestors
have lived and died on these same hills. All of us.
Bahutu, Batutsi, Batwa.
The Hutu listens to the earth and hears things others of
us do not. He is the farmer. Most of Rwanda is Hutu.
To be Tutsi—like me—is to be married to your cattle;
nothing is more valuable than our cows. There are
far fewer of us, but we have always been the proud
descendants of warriors and kings. And there is the
Twa—the little man, the pygmy—who hunts for his
food. But they are fewer still. We are a family. Sharing
a language, a religion, traditions; a past. For me, I have
enough worry just to keep my cows from trampling
Emmanuel's fields. Emmanuel, my old friend, is a
farmer.

(EMMANUEL *can be seen in the distance, working in his field
with his machete.*)

FELICIEN: He knows me so well, sometimes we just sit
together for an afternoon, and we say nothing.

ALPHONSE: *(O S)* Hey, Raymond! Hey, Jackie Chan! Wake up!!

(A worn soccer ball flies onstage, and RAYMOND *stops it with his foot.* ALPHONSE *enters, transistor radio in hand. A shared routine of martial arts moves evolves into dancing.)*

FELICIEN: His grandson, Alphonse, is Raymond's best friend, too.

(A young BOY *runs in, drawn to the radio.)*

FELICIEN: Emmanuel and I, we like to share uragwa— our banana beer—and joke together. He shakes his fist and says,

"Felicien, why must you torment me?! Control those long-horned beasts, or I will have to chop down those skinny Tutsi legs of yours! Then all of us lowly Hutu farmers will celebrate by eating beef for dinner!" "You should be on the radio," I tell him. "You are too funny to waste your time bent over all day in the field!"

(Lights shift.)

ALPHONSE: Did you do it? Did you fix the fan?

RAYMOND: It was just a wire.

ALPHONSE: It was so hot yesterday, Raymond, people were complaining. The only ones who could feel it were in the very front by the television and cassette machine.

RAYMOND: I know. I said already. I am going to find us another fan.

ALPHONSE: And today? What are we showing today?

RAYMOND: *Mad Max* and I have Charles Bronson in *Death Wish 3.*

ALPHONSE: *Blood Sport*?!

RAYMOND: No. There was no Van Damme. We are showing *Commando* again.

ALPHONSE: Shwarzenegger! *(Arnold voice)* "Remember, Sully, when I promised to kill you last?"

ALPHONSE & RAYMOND: "I lied!!!"

(ALPHONSE exits with his radio, the BOY following like a puppy.)

FELICIEN: Hundreds of years ago, our Tutsi ancestors, with their large herds, settled on top of these hills and ruled over the Hutu in their fields and the Twa in the forests below. The stories of our lives together have passed down from generation to generation since time began, entrusted to my family; the story-tellers. My grandson, Raymond? If you look into his eyes, there is a light. A flame. We are connected. He is a story-teller, too.

(RAYMOND joins FELICIEN.)

RAYMOND: Grandfather, I am going away. I will be leaving soon.

FELICIEN: Already I am missing you, just to hear it.

RAYMOND: But you know I would never leave you for very long—I promise I will come back. I want to shoot you.

FELICIEN: Shoot me? Your old grandfather, Felicien, who loves you so much? How could you do such a thing??

RAYMOND: With a camera, Felicien! I want to shoot you with a motion picture camera. I'm going to keep your stories alive.

FELICIEN: They are your stories, too.

RAYMOND: I know. And I'm going to tell them to the world.

FELICIEN: Who put these ideas in your head?

RAYMOND: You did, you crazy old man.

FELICIEN: Me?

RAYMOND: Nyanza!

FELICIEN: Did something happen in Nyanza?

RAYMOND: Here we go, I am being tested.

FELICIEN: No—I know Nyanza, of course, but my old brain loses track. Can you remind me?

RAYMOND: It was a very clear night…

FELICIEN: I told you this?

RAYMOND: Stop it—and you were only a few years older than I am now.

FELICIEN: Who was there?

RAYMOND: Everyone. From miles around.

FELICIEN: Really?

RAYMOND: All waiting together as the sun was going down.

FELICIEN: In Nyanza?

RAYMOND: Old man, I'm going to beat you with your stick!

FELICIEN: What were they waiting for?

RAYMOND: Why do you make me play this game? You know! They put up a big screen in the middle of the road.

FELICIEN: Was it wide?

RAYMOND: I was getting to that. It was a very wide road.

FELICIEN: Details are important.

RAYMOND: The big screen was put up on a very wide road, and the Mwami and his queen—

FELICIEN: Rudahigwa—names are also important.

RAYMOND: Mwami Rudhigawa and his queen arrived in a royal procession. Followed by members of the court, five priests, seven Belgian officials, and a group of Tutsi nobles who appeared as actors in the film. And they all sit in their assigned places in carefully-arranged chairs in front of the screen.

FELICIEN: Very good. I am seeing this now.

RAYMOND: But everyone else—all of you, you said— are sitting in the road. In the dirt. On the other side of the screen. Looking up at it backwards.

FELICIEN: To see it from anywhere, we are happy.

RAYMOND: And a young man from America arrives—

FELICIEN: With boxes.

RAYMOND: I know. Who is telling this story? From a movie studio in America—wearing a suit with all wrinkles, as though he has not slept for weeks—with boxes under his arms.

FELICIEN: And without talking to anyone, he goes straight to work, preparing his machine.

RAYMOND: Oh, so now you remember?

FELICIEN: I was there.

RAYMOND: Then why aren't you telling it? And the machine, when it starts up—

FELICIEN: *(He imitates the sound.)* It chatters. Like a monkey.
And the wheels on top—

RAYMOND: The reels of film begin to turn.

FELICIEN: And out flows a river of light.

RAYMOND: In the middle of nowhere.

FELICIEN: Suddenly, a lion appears. And roars at us.

RAYMOND: It's the M G M lion.

FELICIEN: We are all laughing because we jumped. And then, places we know begin to dance before us. And people—our Watutsi warriors as big as the hills.

RAYMOND: Your very first film.

FELICIEN: We cheer and shout at them.

RAYMOND: *King Solomon's Mines.*

FELICIEN: All made of light.

RAYMOND: In Technicolor.

FELICIEN: Oh, yes—Nyanza! Of course—now I remember!!

RAYMOND: So you see? You are the one who planted this seed in me.

FELICIEN: Do you hear that, Emmanuel? I am planting seeds now. Maybe I am part Hutu.

RAYMOND: Remember last month I told you I was working for a filmmaker? Alan? On his film about the mountain gorillas? Well, he is also a teacher. And he has arranged for me a scholarship.

FELICIEN: A scholarship?

RAYMOND: In New York. I am invited. I am going to learn to make films. You are the first person I am telling. I am going to tell our stories to the world.

(Lights shift. RAYMOND *addresses the audience. An N Y U banner)*

RAYMOND: So, the first time I am holding Alan's camera, I cannot stop smiling. And he starts laughing. "Look at you, Raymond—I think you are in love!" He has me look through the lens, and in my mind, I am already dreaming. He wants to know about me; who I am, what I see. I am full of stories, I tell him. Full of ideas. He talked to me about why he must make films,

and I could see, he, also, was in love. So, I tell him
about Alphonse. How we love movies so much. And
then, about my family and, of course, Felicien. I think,
in all my life I have never talked so much. In Rwanda,
we are very private. But with Alan I am feeling safe.
So, when he offered me to study with him? To learn.
To actually. Do. This? For me—he opened everything.
And Alan and Kate, his wife, they welcomed me. Like
family.

(Lights shift.)

ALAN: Want a bagel? You have to eat something.
Katie? Do we still have any of that Indian food from
last night? Ray says he hasn't eaten. *(To* RAYMOND*)* So,
was I right?

RAYMOND: I am trying to see where he is cutting. Alan,
how does he do this?

ALAN: Hitchcock was a wild man. Whole film's just—
wait, I wrote it down—I have it—Hitchcock—there it
is—ten shots!

RAYMOND: How many books do you have?

ALAN: Notes, Ray! Got to. I figure, if they'd had the
capability, he would've tried to do it in one. But then,
look at *Psycho*—it's all about the cuts. And *Vertigo*?
Insane.

RAYMOND: He moves the camera like—

ALAN: Always pushing the envelope.

RAYMOND: I see. What is 'the envelope?'

ALAN: You know, challenging the boundaries.
Exploring.

RAYMOND: Exploring, yes. I am going to do this, too.

KATE: *(Entering)* Here's some Chicken Vindaloo. You
like spicy, right?

RAYMOND: Oh Kate, thank you!

KATE: Rice here, too—paratha. What'd I miss?

ALAN: Ray's gonna lead the next wave of cinema. The next Kubrick. Did you see my notes on those scenes? They're on—

KATE: Can't look at them right now. That warm enough?

ALAN: I wasn't saying now, just—

RAYMOND: It's fine.

KATE: Why not Truffaut? You need an editor?

ALAN: There's a hot offer!

RAYMOND: Are you serious?

KATE: Just, please—no more gorillas for awhile, okay?

ALAN: You still have to get over there to see them.

KATE: I will.

RAYMOND: Yes, Kate—you have to come!

KATE: I said I will.

ALAN: Not an easy traveller.

KATE: What are you talking about? I'm fine.

RAYMOND: I promise you, you will love it.

KATE: When I'm ready. Hey, did Alan show you what I found for him?

ALAN: The E-bay gods were smiling. Check this out. 1905.

RAYMOND: Another book? You are the book man.

ALAN: About the Belgian Congo, a political pamphlet written as a one-man play. Look a this—King Leopold's Soliloquy. And you know who wrote it? Mark Twain!

KATE: Does he know—?

RAYMOND: Huckleberry—is this really a name?

KATE: How do you—?

ALAN: Too much time together in the mountains.

RAYMOND: Life on the Mississippi.

KATE: Oh, my god.

ALAN: The horrors of this guy. Photographs of all these people with their hands cut off. A real call to action.

RAYMOND: The Belgians, yes. They came also to Rwanda.

KATE: Really enticing.

ALAN: Almost a hundred years ago. Relax.

KATE: Just saying. I like places I can drive to.

ALAN: Anyway, nobody wanted to hear it. Even his own publisher.

RAYMOND: Alphonse says, we can call Our first movie Life on the Nyabarongo!

KATE: Gotta meet this guy.

ALAN: What time is it? Don't you have to take your dad—?

KATE: What time—oh, shit—appointment's at five. Why are all his doctors on the Upper East Side? Please don't let me be stuck with that man in rush hour traffic again.

RAYMOND: He is all right?

ALAN: Sharp as a tack, just gets impatient.

KATE: But the rest of him's falling apart.

ALAN: Hope I'm that together at eighty seven. You better move it.

KATE: Thank you— Yes, I know. I'm going! Purse, keys, scarf, gloves…

ALAN: Head…

KATE: Shut up. I'll call you. (*She exits.*)

RAYMOND: Will she come?

ALAN: She hasn't flown since—whatever. She'll figure
it out. Hey, 'global information-sharing.' You hear
about this? On the computer. Now they're calling it
The World Wide Web. Ray—damn!—we're all getting
closer.

(RAYMOND *turns back to the audience.*)

RAYMOND: I am not a stranger to death. Ten years
ago—April of my second year in New York—I will
always remember. Film history. Watching *Birth of a
Nation.* In the darkness, I feel a hand on my shoulder.
It's Alan. Something is wrong. We go quickly to
his apartment. On the news they are talking about
Rwanda. Someone has shot down the president's
plane, and my country has exploded.

(*Light shift to* ALAN *and* KATE'*s apartment.*)

ALAN: So, why is no-one being sent? We must be doing
something!

KATE: I don't know, Alan. Maybe one of the other
channels has more information.

ALAN: And they say it so matter-of-factly.

KATE: Really frustrating. Raymond, is there someone
you want to call?

ALAN: He's the head of the U N peace-keepers, for
god's sake—our guy on the ground, who sees what's
going on—and he's calling for reinforcements. What
the fuck?

KATE: Where's Clinton in all of this? Come on, Bill, step
up! Try C N N again.

ALAN: They don't have anything either. "Sudden mass hysterical grief and violence", they said.

KATE: Because their president was killed?

ALAN: Nobody's telling us. There has to be something we can do.

KATE: Raymond, who can we call? We need to check on your family.

RAYMOND: *(To us)* Through it all, I am very still, but my heart is pounding like a drum.

ALAN: If I could just Look out through his eyes. See what he's seeing.

KATE: What's the international code for Rwanda?

ALAN: 'Tribal violence' is just code for "they're not like us." Come on. Gangs are tribal. The Mafia. Sorry, Ray, I'll shut up. This must be so crazy for you. You all right?

KATE: Here's the phone.

RAYMOND: *(To us)* But the lines are all busy. Or perhaps they are down. Finally, four days later, I reach one of my cousins in Kigali. He has not seen any of my sisters or Alphonse, but he has spoken with Felicien. "Do not come back," he says. "It is not safe." And when I do return, a few months later, after the fighting is over? Alan comes with me. What we saw—I cannot begin to tell you—it was. Beyond the imagination. Way beyond. May you never see anything like this. Never.
From my family—no one is left. Together, we begin to collect their stories. What has happened to each of them.
Eventually we learn them all. All but one. Still I cannot find what has happened to my grandfather, Felicien. Ten years now I am looking. But every day I hear his voice.

When Alan finally left, we both knew he would be back.

It had gotten inside him. So, when Kate contacted me to tell me. This. I lost my breath. And, of course, I must be here.

(Lights shift. A N Y C apartment)

KATE: *(Off stage)* Water's on. Do you want some tea?

RAYMOND: I should be making it for you.

KATE: *(Off stage)* We still have some you brought us.

RAYMOND: Rwanda tea?

KATE: *(Entering)* No, Raymond—English Breakfast.

RAYMOND: Sometimes, Kate, you are Whoopi Goldberg. *(Beat)* You are very kind to wait for me to get a visa.

KATE: No way I was doing it without you. That was beautiful—what you said.

RAYMOND: It was the truth.

KATE: He loved you. *(Giving him tea)* Careful. Hot.

RAYMOND: Thank you. I am needing this.

KATE: He came home—different—ten years ago, Raymond. From Rwanda.

RAYMOND: I know. We saw a lot.

KATE: Couldn't talk about it. He'd start, but then… Of course, you heard about the peacekeeper they wouldn't listen to. The Canadian.

RAYMOND: Dallaire.

KATE: Found him under some park bench a few years later. Really affected Alan. Become completely obsessed with him. Said he could understand. But with Alan it was his heart that gave out. He couldn't sleep, you know? Once he got back. Never a problem before.

Stay up reading or on the computer. Taking notes, making lists. Gathering up the pieces.

RAYMOND: Humpty Dumpty.

KATE: Yeah. He told you. So, now what, Raymond?

(Pause)

RAYMOND: Flying in over the city was very strange—

KATE: How do you mean?

RAYMOND: Without the towers.

KATE: Oh, right. And that. A lot has changed.

(Lights find FELICIEN *on his hill.)*

FELICIEN: The world is not the same now. I watched when the Devil came to visit these thousand hills, this heaven on earth. I prayed to Imana, soul of the earth and sky and trees and rivers, to give me strength to continue watching even when I wanted to close my eyes and remember only the past. Because someone must tell the children who were not yet born, who did not see. Someone must tell them the truth about what happened.

(Lights return us to KATE *and* RAYMOND.*)*

RAYMOND: Near the end of the killing, many people saw him.

KATE: And he was fine. What about his friend—the farmer?

RAYMOND: Emmanuel?

KATE: He must know something.

RAYMOND: When the killing began, Emmanuel hid one of my sisters and her children in the ceiling of his house. He knew he was risking his life.

KATE: What happened?

RAYMOND: It is very difficult to keep children quiet. *(Beat)* For ten years now, in my own country, still I cannot settle.

KATE: What about Alphonse?

RAYMOND: He was one of the people. He saw him there. Alphonse. We were supposed to make films together. When I got back.

KATE: Can't you still?

RAYMOND: Now, it is complicated.

KATE: What do you mean?

RAYMOND: So many are in prison.

KATE: Alphonse?

RAYMOND: Anyone can accuse you. And if you were with the wrong people...

KATE: That's terrible. Do you visit him?

RAYMOND: Of course. And if you are knowing him—he has done nothing. But there is such a long wait for a trial.
It can take years. I have spoken to many people on his behalf, but each one sends me on to someone else.

KATE: So, he's just stuck there?

RAYMOND: I keep trying.

KATE: What a nightmare.

(The deafening sound of a plane taking off directly overhead. Its shadow darkens the stage.)

FELICIEN: Me, I am not a rich man—only a few cows of my own—it brings bad luck to say the number. Sometimes we mix our herds together, disguising who has how many, to avoid the resentment large numbers might bring. But in my lifetime, to be Tutsi came to mean that you are wealthy. So in truth, I would not be considered very Tutsi.

(A bull bellows O S.)

FELICIEN: Do not be angry, Rugira, I am talking only about numbers! You and Ingizi are my eternal pride and joy. *(Back to us)* But I am very rich in stories. One story I can tell you is about a muzungu; a white man who came here, he said, to protect us. But he did not know us.

(Lights reveal the interior of an airport motel room somewhere in the midwestern United States. A fresh floral arrangement sits on a table, full-length drapes cover the windows.)

KATE: *(To* RAYMOND*)* Turns out, that guy, Dallaire, survived the whole park bench thing. Now he travels around speaking about his experiences. Even went on to write a book. Alan read it, of course. Several times. Scoured it.

RAYMOND: The bookman.

KATE: And everything else he could find; interviews, articles, websites, blogs. Like he's looking for an answer.

RAYMOND: It gets inside you.

(Mozart's Requiem in D Minor *begins to play from the bedside clock radio.)*

KATE: He'd started to dream about Dallaire, did I tell you? These long, involved surreal journeys. After awhile, it was all he could talk about. Now, anytime his name comes up, I just see Alan.

(The door opens and MAJOR GENERAL ROMEO DALLAIRE *[played by the same actor who played* ALAN*] is led into the room by a white* BELLMAN.*)*

BELLMAN: I have to tell you, sir, we were all waiting to see if you'd show up in uniform.

DALLAIRE: I'm retired.

BELLMAN: My wife—she read your book, you know?—
won't leave me alone about you. Said it's fantastic—

(A strange sound begins which only we and DALLAIRE
hear.)

DALLAIRE: Oh, yes?

BELLMAN: You're the real thing, she says; a real hero!
Hey, I have to tell you, they put you in my favorite
room. Right on the corner.

(As the BELLMAN *opens the drapes,* DALLAIRE *turns,
sensing something. A Rwandan* WOMAN *in a dark raincoat
enters and looks at him. Only* DALLAIRE *sees her.)*

BELLMAN: So, you really been through it all, huh?!

(The radio switches to lively African music. The WOMAN
hums along.)

BELLMAN: Just hackin' each other up? Their own
neighbors, right? I have to read it. She said you looked
in their eyes, and like, saw the devil. Nothin' but evil.

(The BOY *from the beginning, wearing a dirty windbreaker,
enters, stops, and looks at* DALLAIRE.)

BELLMAN: Hey—sorry. Talkin' your ear off here, and
you just landed—but she'll lit'rally kill me if I don't—

*(*BELLMAN *pulls out a copy of* DALLAIRE'*s book. As the* BOY
continues to stare, the WOMAN *lights a candle and takes it
into the bathroom.)*

BELLMAN: If you could just—her name's Marci—this'll
mean a lot to her—with an "I".

*(*DALLAIRE *signs it and hands it back, as we hear the shower
go on.)*

BELLMAN: Just saved my life, sir. Can't tell you. So the
guys doing all the killing over there—the Tutus?

DALLAIRE: The Hutu. The Hutu were in power—the
Hutu and the Tutsi.

(Wah-Wah Tusi by the Orlons begins to play. The WOMAN *returns, as steam rolls with her out of the bathroom.)*

BELLMAN: You see the flowers, sir? Big deal having a hero in town—a real honor!

(The WOMAN *begins to unbutton her raincoat.)*

DALLAIRE: I just—

BELLMAN: Yeah, yeah, yeah, sorry—my bad. Just hang this in the closet for you, and I'm outta here. Oh, and here's your key, General. For the mini-bar.

DALLAIRE: No, I don't want that in here.

(The WOMAN *removes her coat, revealing a once-white slip, caked with dirt and blood. As she returns to the bathroom, closing the door, the* BOY *lies down on the bed in an unnatural position.)*

BELLMAN: I know what you mean. They charge you an arm and a leg.

(The sound of whispers)

DALLAIRE: *(To the boy)* Why are you back?

BELLMAN: Sorry?

DALLAIRE: Why?

BELLMAN: Me, sir?

DALLAIRE: I thought we were done.

BELLMAN: Don't want to bother you.

DALLAIRE: Maybe I should have just—

(A woman's scream in his head.)

BELLMAN: Pool's open 'til ten, no lifeguard after eight. The ice machine—

DALLAIRE: Nothing's simple. Too many rules.

BELLMAN: I know. I'll put out the "Do Not Disturb." If you need anything else, sir, my name is Larry.

(Sound of a small jet close overhead. DALLAIRE *flinches. The woman's scream again, this time closer, then multiplies and grows.)*

DALLAIRE: I stayed—you saw me. You would have been—what?—completely—What do you want?

LARRY: Sir? Are you all right?

DALLAIRE: It's just too much.

LARRY: I'll check back, okay? *(He exits.)*

DALLAIRE: Too. Much. What I needed. I told them repeatedly. Was. Exactly what. Wouldn't listen. I asked for. Everything: soldiers, vehicles, spare parts, bullets, you know?—I couldn't even—Not to mention permission—PERMISSION to—give us some desks even, chairs, maybe paper? You know, paper CLIPS would even help. That's it. That's all. Some help. Just help us—Someone. For god's sake, women and children— *(He pulls out a pill bottle, checks the label. To the* BOY*)* What? What are you looking at? Son, you have no idea—I tried. I was trying to get their— ATTENTION. I was there to protect you. But all of us, we all needed help.

(A larger plane passes over, rattling the room. On the bed, The BOY's *limbs begin to move slightly.* DALLAIRE *pulls a fifth of vodka out of his bag and opens the pill bottle.)*

FELICIEN: In Rwanda we say, once you visit, you will always be coming back. Something here gets inside you.

(The radio suddenly goes on by itself.)

D J's VOICE: And now, one of my favorites; Mozart's Requiem in D Minor.

(The first movement begins to play. Lights return us to KATE *and* RAYMOND.)*

KATE: Something, he said, you had found online.

RAYMOND: The most amazing story.

KATE: Alan loved how you'd framed it.

RAYMOND: It's a confession. Of a man in prison.

KATE: Felt like he'd seen the film just reading your screenplay. So, tell me about it.

RAYMOND: Really? You want to hear? It starts with a great wide Hollywood crane shot.

KATE: First shot and there goes the budget.

RAYMOND: We glide slowly through the clouds, down toward the earth to discover a building with big walls around it. Moving closer and closer until we find a man looking out the window of his cell. Focusing tighter. One man alone.

KATE: So, is everyone in prison?

RAYMOND: In Rwanda, there are many, yes. But Thomas, he is in Mali. For the international court. Thomas Sibomana. He is one of the big fish.

(THOMAS SIBOMANA, *a middle-aged Rwandan bureaucrat, stands at his window. It is uncomfortably hot.*)

RAYMOND: Read this.

KATE: "I, Thomas Sibomana, having pleaded my guilty conscience at the so-called African Nuremberg and now sitting in jail in Mali—" Sounds well-educated.

RAYMOND: Keep going.

(THOMAS *now speaks to us.*)

THOMAS: I tell this story because now ten years have passed and already it is largely forgotten. The world cries out "Never Again", but Rwanda, it seems, is less memorable. Partly due to pigment, of course, but also because our lovely land of one thousand hills has no oil other than sesame oil. Not even many diamonds. And because America's last glimpse of Africa was the shocking images of G I Joe dragged through the streets of Mogadishu, like a martyred Crusading saint. Heroically memorialized in Hollywood wide-screen.

KATE: Is that *Blackhawk Down*?

RAYMOND: Ridley Scott; *Alien, Gladiator, Blade Runner.* Keep going.

THOMAS: Where is the movie of Rwanda? A crime so immense, apparently it cannot be filmed and has no audience.

RAYMOND: So, I read this, and I thought, me—I'll do it. I'll make the movie of Rwanda. And I will make it about him.

THOMAS: On paper, according to the indictment and my guilty plea, I am a genocidaire, which, I assure you, fills me with disgust and self-hatred. But when I look into my heart—I don't think it's true. A broken landscape littered with irony. My lawyers had a legal defense, of course, but I also have a moral one. Or should I say personal. I have loved Tutsi in my life. How then can I be charged with desiring their extinction as a people?

KATE: "I have loved Tutsi in my life"?

RAYMOND: That's our story. That's Cat-reen.

WOMAN'S VOICE: *(Off stage)* AAARGH!!! *(Scream)* WHAT KIND OF MAN ARE YOU?!

RAYMOND: Two men have cornered a ten year-old boy. One carries a club, the other a panga—a machete.

(The same WOMAN and BOY from DALLAIRE's hotel room.)

CAT-REEN: WHAT KIND OF MAN THREATENS A BOY?! YOU SHOULD BE ASHAMED!

RAYMOND: She blocks their way. Thomas appears in the doorway.

CAT-REEN: WHO RAISED YOU TO DO THIS? YOU ARE NOT MEN! PLEASE—SOMEONE! IN THE NAME OF GOD—WHERE IS YOUR HUMANITY?!

RAYMOND: He has never seen a woman so brave.

CAT-REEN: DON'T YOU DARE—DON'T YOU PUSH ME! YOU WILL NOT TOUCH HIM!!

RAYMOND: The panga rises up to strike—

CAT-REEN: YOU WILL HAVE TO KILL ME, TOO!

RAYMOND: —and she grabs the blade with her bare hand.

KATE: Oh, my god!

THOMAS: NO! STOP THIS! STOP! RIGHT NOW! ARE YOU INSANE? WHAT ARE YOU DOING?!

CAT-REEN: THEY ARE WANTING TO KILL HIM!!

THOMAS: OUT OF HERE—BOTH OF YOU! NOW!! DO YOU HEAR ME? RIGHT NOW!!! I WILL HAVE YOU ARRESTED! DON'T EVEN DARE TO THINK OF FACING ME!

RAYMOND: They take off running.

THOMAS: YOU'D BETTER RUN! *(To her)* Take him inside. *(To them)* I AM WATCHING YOU! KEEP GOING. I WILL FIND OUT WHERE YOU LIVE, AND TEACH YOU ABOUT FEAR! YOU ARE NOT MEN!!

(Lights. Inside, the WOMAN *holds the* BOY, THOMAS' *napkin wrapped tightly around her hand.* THOMAS *enters.)*

CAT-REEN: Cowards! I will show them!!

THOMAS: They would have killed you!

CAT-REEN: All those people watching—doing nothing!?

THOMAS: Let me see your hand.

CAT-REEN: I'm fine. They should be ashamed!

THOMAS: It's deep. We need a doctor.

He nods to the waiter who runs out.

CAT-REEN: But you—who are you? You are not afraid.
Thank God!

THOMAS: You need to keep it higher than your heart, or
you'll bleed all over. You— What were you thinking?
(He falls into his chair, shaking.)

CAT-REEN: Dear my God, are you hurt, too?

THOMAS: No, I am just—I am not a man of action.

CAT-REEN: But just now you were so brave. They ran.
You saved us.

THOMAS: I am no James Bond.

CAT-REEN: Well,—then you are even braver. You dear,
dear man!

(CAT-REEN gives THOMAS a drink of water.)

THOMAS: Your son—is he all right?

CAT-REEN: This boy? I've never seen him.

THOMAS: What?

CAT-REEN: He is not mine. I am not married.

THOMAS: My god—you're even madder than I thought.

CAT-REEN: But you do not know me, either. So, who is
mad?

THOMAS: Then, allow me to introduce myself. Thomas
Sibomana.

CAT-REEN: And I am Cat-reen Bunyanyezi.

THOMAS: Like Cat-reen the Great?

CAT-REEN: Like Cat-reen my grandmother.

THOMAS: No—I think you are more like Cat-reen
Deneuve.

CAT-REEN: You will make me shy.

THOMAS: Shy? I do not think so. No, I think those men are the ones I saved—from you!

(THOMAS *rewraps* CAT-REEN's *hand with a clean dish towel brought over by the* WAITER. *He also brings a bottle of Guinness which he opens in front of them, then whispers something to* THOMAS.)

THOMAS: He says the doctor is on his way. Cheers.

CAT-REEN: To my hero.

THOMAS: No, to mine!

(CAT-REEN *and* THOMAS *drink.*)

CAT-REEN: Where is your family?

THOMAS: My mother died in childbirth—that is, having me. And I was never sure who my father was. But the man who raised me encouraged me to study. "Learn everything you can," he said. It was not available to Hutu of his generation. Why am I telling you all this?

CAT-REEN: You are still shaking.

THOMAS: I'm fine.

CAT-REEN: This man, where is he now?

THOMAS: He died while I was still in university. A sad man. A drunk.

CAT-REEN: No brother or sisters?

THOMAS: Only me.

CAT-REEN: I am the same. Only me. Me and my mother now. You are married?

THOMAS: Yes. One daughter; nine years old. We live in Paris.

CAT-REEN: Oh, Paris. Oh, I see. So far away. And is that your car?

THOMAS: The black one—yes—with the flags and official stickers?

CAT-REEN: Mister Government man. And yet, you saved my life.

THOMAS: I am not the government.

CAT-REEN: No. I see much more. You are a rare man. A very good man.

THOMAS: Cat-reen, your eyes. The deepest wells I have ever looked into.

CAT-REEN: Do you say this to all the Tutsi girls?

THOMAS: No, please—I have never said this. Even to my wife.

CAT-REEN: That is not good.

THOMAS: We are friends, I mean, but we married very young.

CAT-REEN: (Long beat) I am not one to go with a married man.

THOMAS: Cat-reen la Bunyanyezi.

CAT-REEN: But I do not want you to leave.

THOMAS: "Each time dawn appears,—"

CAT-REEN: "—the mystery is there in its entirety."

THOMAS: You know it?

CAT-REEN: Rene Daumal. My father used to—he loved poetry.

(THOMAS smiles.)

CAT-REEN: What?

THOMAS: I need to see you again.

CAT-REEN: You will.

THOMAS: But these are dangerous times.

CAT-REEN: Your wife…

THOMAS: Yes?

CAT-REEN: She is a very lucky woman.

(Lights change.)

KATE: So, this is great—what happens? So full of contradictions.

RAYMOND: He confides in us—right into the lens.

(Lights change.)

THOMAS: It was not power I wanted, it was knowledge. And experience. I thirsted for these. And in return, it seems, signed away my soul. But, I believe, it was Goethe who said, that "he who constantly strives can always be saved".
So, I rewind my life in fits and starts, editing for the high points, trying to see where, if ever, I had a choice...

(Lights out on THOMAS, as RAYMOND puts down the manuscript.)

RAYMOND: "What is true love? And how far would I go to protect it?" He wrestles with every step: "How much am I willing to sacrifice? How honest do I dare to be? With her? And with myself?" And we come to know him, "warts and all".

KATE: I see why Alan got so excited.

RAYMOND: You see, for Rwanda this man—this Thomas Sibomana—he is something new—a Hutu aristocrat. When he was very young, he got a girl pregnant on their second date. He is honorable, so he marries her. She turns out to be a distant cousin of the president's wife.

KATE: The president's wife? Alan talked about her. The real power, he said.

RAYMOND: Yes—Madame Agathe. She and her brothers; the "Clan de Madame." The Akazu. So

Thomas is very smart, very capable, and the President notices. Makes him his special loan arranger...

KATE: Like finance minister, you mean?

RAYMOND: Yes, but then he also makes him his spinner of the press. In Paris. To put a good face on Rwanda.

KATE: So clearly, he trusts him.

RAYMOND: And finally, he wants Thomas to be his official historian. His Hutu historian. To counter the traditional version—the Tutsi version.

KATE: Whoever wins...

RAYMOND: Exactly. He even has his own radio show. A regular 'fireside chat' with the people of Rwanda.

(THOMAS *puts on headphones, a microphone appears, and a French "ON THE AIR" sign lights up. A* D J *sets up nearby.*)

THOMAS: ...because for hundreds of years, the Tutsi ruled Rwanda, and they held the Hutu down. It's a historical fact. They held us down. If we didn't obey, we were beaten. But not killed, of course—they needed us. Because we did all the work! And that is why, in 1959, we had our Hutu Rebellion. France had their own Peasant Uprising which is now famous across the world! It was the best of times. My Hutu brothers, I wish you and your families God's blessings and Imana's. This is Thomas Sibomana wishing you good night.

(*As* THOMAS *takes off the headphones, the* D J *takes over.*)

D J: Mr. Minister tells you the historical facts! THEY. HELD. US. DOWN! Look at their long legs—and their little nose which they look down so arrogant at us! They care more for their precious cows than for the Hutu. Look closely at their little nose—then BREAK IT!

(*Lights on* FELICIEN)

FELICIEN: The most listened-to—and entertaining—station in the country was R T L M—Radio Television Libre des Milles Collines. Created to feed the fire when things were at their worst. Sometimes called "Radio-Télé La Mort"…or "Vampire Radio".

D J: Hey, Mister Minister! *(Raising a fist)* I Hate These Hutu!

(THOMAS nods, returns the "Power" gesture, and exits. I Hate These Hutu plays.)

FELICIEN: And all the best music! Every day they would play this song by Simon Bikindi; *I Hate These Hutu.* Over and over. Not against the Hutu, as it sounds, but about the Hutu who wanted to live side by side with the Tutsi. The ones who had not learned from the past. And everyone—even the Tutsi—sang along. We drank and laughed together.

(Lights on KATE and RAYMOND.)

KATE: So, he's calling for violence against the Tutsi and at the same time, he's in love with one.

RAYMOND: This is Rwanda—full of contradictions and ready to explode.

(Rolling thunder, as lights shift to DALLAIRE taking a long pull on his bottle.)

FELICIEN: A sleeping volcano, silent for a hundred years, may suddenly awaken in anger.

(A MAN's voice comes from behind the drapes.)

MAN'S VOICE: That's enough! Put it down, ya damn fool!!

(DALLAIRE sits up.)

DALLAIRE: Alo?

MAN'S VOICE: Don't move a damn muscle! D'you hear!!

(A flash of lightning, the drapes move.)

DALLAIRE: Who's there?

(Stillness. Then suddenly—)

MAN'S VOICE: JEALOUS BASTARDS! FILTHY HYPOCRITES!! If I HAD THEM BY THE THROAT!!!

(—they burst open, revealing a figure with blinding backlight. As he comes forward, we see a man with a large beard, a long, elegant, frock coat, and an ornate crucifix around his neck.)

MAN/KING LEOPOLD: Of course their hands have been chopped off. What do they expect? Lazy savages! One missionary sees eighty-one of them drying over a fire and decides to set it down in print, the worthless bastard, accusing me of mutilations, murders, massacres! Me!! Leopold, King of Belgium, Emperor of the Belgian Congo, Benefactor of a downtrodden and friendless people! So I am forced to suppress it!!! But then, along comes the most powerful enemy that has ever confronted us, the Kodak—the incorruptible Kodak—and all that harmony goes to hell!

(The sound of a camera click, and a black and white photo is projected of a Congolese native missing a hand. More clicks, more photos.)

(MAN/LEOPOLD tosses away his costume and beard, revealing MARK TWAIN, in his iconic white suit.)

MAN/MARK TWAIN: Ah! Caught you—good!! 'Fraid I'd lost my timing! Now, stop this damn fool nonsense immediately! *(Lights his trademark cigar)*

DALLAIRE: Wait—I know you.

MARK TWAIN: Well, that's mildly reassuring—been out of circulation awhile. But you cannot depend on your eyes when your imagination is out of focus. Now, cease and desist!

DALLAIRE: Of course! You're—I know you. You're—

MARK TWAIN: Dead?

DALLAIRE: No, famous! You're—oh shit—Mark Twain?!

MARK TWAIN: Guilty as charged.

DALLAIRE: *Tom Sawyer. Pudd'nhead Wilson!*

MARK TWAIN: No small victory, you know—to be remembered in the tide of Times! To have lived that when we die even the undertaker is sorry! You, sir, are a goddamn fool!

DALLAIRE: But wait, so, what are you—an actor?

MARK TWAIN: Unfortunately, merely an amateur. However, you mustn't mistake my response for humility; no sir—it is purely convenience. I've simply discovered, you see, that if I tell the truth, I don't have to remember so much. Also a damn sight easier to confess these things "post mortem".

DALLAIRE: So, you really are—

MARK TWAIN: Yup. As a doornail. Quite dearly departed.

(DALLAIRE *looks at the pill bottle.*)

DALLAIRE: So, it's over? I'm done?

MARK TWAIN: I'm told that's still not been decided.

DALLAIRE: Not decided? But aren't you—?

MARK TWAIN: Your River Styx boatman? No, nothin' like that. I'm more of an ally. Have to pardon my 'Deus Ex Machina' entrance, but they almost never allow us these crossovers. So I thought, "What the hell— Carpe damn Diem! Why not give'im a little heavenly spectacle!" Called in more than a few favors to get here, but— "*voila!*" Finally agreed to let me accompany you through your final review.

DALLAIRE: Review? You mean, there's more?

MARK TWAIN: Your life's a-hangin', sir, in the proverbial balance. Razor's edge. But decision's still yours to make. In your hands, General. A matter of will.

DALLAIRE: So, I'm still—

MARK TWAIN: Look, I'm just here to escort you. Got opinions on everything, of course, but don't worry—I won't keep'em to myself. Sure hope this don't turn out to be a wasted trip. Put a lot of damn effort into getting here!

DALLAIRE: My mother appeared to me once, but— Mark Twain.

MARK TWAIN: Watched your African adventure from the best seat in the house. Infuriated me all over again. Came here to persuade you to stay the course, sir. A man of conscience is a precious commodity. And a hell of a lot left to be done!

DALLAIRE: Leave me alone. I thought you wrote comedies.

MARK TWAIN: When I learned about the horrors of the Congo, it damn well drained the comedy right outta me. And same as you—tried like hell to arouse the world's attention, but—

DALLAIRE: I'm done with that now. Good lord, my head is—

MARK TWAIN: Pills'n'liquor, General—the Devil's cocktail! Summons up a dense fog on your river! Truth is, worst loneliness in the world, of course, is not to be comfortable with yourself.

DALLAIRE: Never had Mark Twain before.

MARK TWAIN: And you're not gonna get him again, either, so don't waste this golden opportunity—clock's a-tickin'.

DALLAIRE: Go away.

MARK TWAIN: (*Puts a finger to his lips*) Save your energy, sir. No word was ever as effective as a rightly-timed pause.

DALLAIRE: I can't—

MARK TWAIN: Don't worry, sir—I'm on watch now. Rough waters ahead, but I'm here to help you navigate. I am the reinforcements you've been calling for, dead man's honor—I am the goddamned cavalry!

(DALLAIRE *collapses.* MARK TWAIN *snaps his fingers, and suddenly, sirens wail and flashing lights fill the stage.*)

(KATE *and* RAYMOND *back at the apartment.*)

KATE: We'd actually made plans to come over.

RAYMOND: To Rwanda? Both of you? Seriously?!

KATE: For the ten-year commemoration. We wanted to surprise you.

RAYMOND: That's in two weeks!

KATE: Had our tickets, shots, everything. He almost made it.

RAYMOND: I am just so happy to know you would come. But now—

KATE: So, I'm walking up Ninth avenue, last week, headed up to my editing room to put the stuff together for the memorial, totally depressed, and I come across a group of pre-schoolers out on a field trip, hanging onto separate loops along a rope—you've seen those, right? Like ten or twelve of them being guided along by three adults—New York City thing. And they've come to a stop near the intersection, and one of their

teachers, this young guy—is up at the corner watching
the traffic, waiting for the light. And just as I pass, this
one little boy—maybe three or four—cranes his neck,
to see what's going on, sighs loudly and says, "C'mon
Dave, we're not getting any younger!"

RAYMOND: You made Alan laugh so hard one time he
almost peed.

KATE: He damn well did. Had to change his pants.

RAYMOND: You are too much. "C'mon Dave."

KATE: Ray, I need to do this.

RAYMOND: You mean you will come? Just you?

KATE: Well, I was thinking you'd come, too.

RAYMOND: No, of course!

KATE: And besides, after all those shots—I'm not
wasting that.

RAYMOND: Finally you will see my country. Kate, now
I will show you Rwanda!

(FELICIEN *appears.*)

FELICIEN: For thirty years, some of our Tutsi cousins
have been living in Uganda, to the north, as refugees.
They train with the Ugandan rebels and help to
overthrow their dictator. Then, the new Ugandan
president says to them, "Go back where you belong.
We will give you guns, but you must fight your own
fight—you are Rwandese!"

(*A loud verbal military call to assemble, as men in
R P F uniforms race in from all sides, falling into a tight
formation.*)

R P F SOLDIERS: Well then, Rwanda—HERE. (*Clap, clap*)
WE. (*Clap, clap*) COME! (*Clap, clap, clap*)

FELICIEN: They say they are coming back to liberate our
hillsides. But after thirty years, many of us here, we no

longer know these cousins. So even to many of us, it's
an invasion.

(The R P F SOLDIERS *start their song again.)*

D J: The R P F are coming, my Hutu brothers! We must
stop the inyenzi before it becomes an infestation!!
Thirty years ago, we finally threw the Tutsi aristocracy
off our backs, and now their children are wanting to
return!!!

(The singing continues, as R P F SOLDIERS *do an
impressive, well-coordinated drill.)*

D J: They wish to dominate us. To return us to slavery!
We must all protect Rwanda from these *Inyenzi
Inkotanyi*!

(THOMAS *speaks to the lens.)*

THOMAS: "*Inyenzi*." It means cockroach. That's what
all of us called them. That was used against every one
of us in the trials, of course. And there's the irony,
you see? Because the R P F, themselves, were the first
to coin the term. "*Inyenzi*" was their expression for
themselves.

R P F SOLDIER: We make night-time raids across the
border, in and out—can't stop us. Like "*inyenzi*".

THOMAS: If, instead, we called them "cocker
spaniels"—would it then have been a "civil war" and
not a "genocide"?

R P F SOLDIER: We will finally liberate Rwanda from
Hutu control! R P F!!! *(He exits.)*

THOMAS: All of us in Habyarimana's government are
busy packing our bags. The deal is done. The rebels are
battle-trained and well-supplied. The writing, as they
say, is on the wall. Just another shift of power. Tutsi
in, Hutu out. So it goes. History is full of them. And
everything would have been different. No genocide,

no trials, no infamy. But instead, Haby picks up the
phone and makes a desperate call to Paris. The Africa
office. One call and together we begin our mythological
descent. Into Hell.

(FELICIEN *speaks from his hill.*)

FELICIEN: The first muzungu who came here were the
Germans. We liked the Germans. Very organized.
Though we pitied their baby skin. We are organized,
too, so they kept our system. But when the Belgians
came to replace them, they divided us. Measured
our noses and foreheads, looked at our teeth, and
proclaimed the Tutsi superior. More intelligent. More
like them. We were more white. And they pushed us to
be tougher with the Hutu. Then, came the French.

(*A* FRENCH OFFICIAL *appears in a separate light, hanging
up a phone as he talks.*)

FRENCH OFFICIAL: A French-speaking country under
attack by English-speaking rebels? We cannot tolerate
another loss to our cultural influence in Africa!

RAYMOND: Their grandparents all spoke French, but
the R P F soldiers grew up in Uganda, so they all speak
English!

FRENCH OFFICIAL: *Vive le Francophonie!!*

RAYMOND: The chess game for Africa between the
French and the English.

FRENCH OFFICIAL: We are sending the Foreign Legion!!!

FELICIEN: Then, there is a man—a very dangerous
man—named Bagasora. Colonel Theoneste Bagasora.

(BAGASORA *appears in full uniform.*)

BAGASORA: The Inyenzi will not engage with an
international superpower. They are too clever for that.
They will simply pull back and wait for the French
to leave. So, we must prepare for that day. I have a

strategy. As clear as the Hutu nose on my face. We are eight million people in Rwanda. And seven million Hutu. The Chinese say, "Many hands make light work."

THOMAS: The Chinese have provided us with many things. Amahoro Stadium, the road to Ruhengeri, and one machete for every three men in Rwanda.

BAGASORA: We will arm and train our Hutu men to weed out all collaborators. We must prepare for the apocalypse!

THOMAS: Haby calls in the U N to freeze the situation.

BAGASORA: The United Nations are idiots.

THOMAS: And this is when Rwanda meets Dallaire.

(The final bars of Canada's national anthem. Sounds of a large, enthusiastic crowd and the roar of artillery, as DALLAIRE *appears at a podium in full dress uniform.)*

DALLAIRE: As we celebrate twenty-five years of excellence, the thunder of our cannons rolling across the Plains of Abraham reminds me what an honor it is to be guarding these great stone walls of Quebec City, training the finest artillery soldiers in Canada, and preparing tomorrow's peacekeepers!

(Loud cheers)

DALLAIRE: This is a great day for our school, for our country, and for the world. *Allons-y!*

(Shouts of "Allons-y!", huge applause and another cannon roar.)

DALLAIRE: Also, I have an announcement to make. I recently received a phone call offering me my first command of a United Nations peacekeeping mission overseas. As soldiers, I am sure you understand; this is what we wait our whole lives for—what many of us would kill our own mothers for, God rest her soul. So, of course, I have accepted.

(Lights change. MARK TWAIN appears.)

MARK TWAIN: Your own mother?

DALLAIRE: Go away, will you?! Why am I here?

MARK TWAIN: Perspective, sir. As I told you, it's a review. So, all of your training, you say, had been leading to this?

DALLAIRE: My own mission?! A mission command?! Of course!

MARK TWAIN: Well, *"Allons-y!"* Self-sacrifice. To content a soldier's spirit.

DALLAIRE: I went to assist and protect a people in need.

MARK TWAIN: And to content yourself, of course.

DALLAIRE: Something wrong with that?

MARK TWAIN: No, nothing at all. In fact—bright eyes, full of energy and out to make a difference in the world? Why, we should bottle that and sell it door to door! But were you familiar with the region?

DALLAIRE: No. I knew nothing at all. I was diving in the dark.

MARK TWAIN: So, you left your family to lead a group of men you'd never met and protect the people of some distant country you knew nothing about?

(The BOY appears and looks at DALLAIRE.)

DALLAIRE: That's what I was trained to do.

MARK TWAIN: That settles it, then—off we go!

DALLAIRE: What? Off we—to where?

MARK TWAIN: To the source.

DALLAIRE: I am not going back.

MARK TWAIN: Filled with purpose,

DALLAIRE: No, I'm—

MARK TWAIN: Poised for success.

DALLAIRE: Stop it. I can't—

MARK TWAIN: No need to worry.

DALLAIRE: Don't make me go back there!

MARK TWAIN: Deep breath, sir—and onward!

(The BOY *reaches out his hand. Cheering and lights of the ceremony)*

DALLAIRE: Gentlemen, I am headed for Africa.

(More cheering and:)

ALL: *Allons-y!*

(The roar of artillery)

(Blackout)

END OF ACT ONE

ACT TWO

FELICIEN: Since he is a little boy, Raymond has always been curious. Why this, Grandfather? Why that? "Why do you test the depth of the water with your foot?" "Because," I would answer, "only a fool will test it with both feet!" "Grandfather, you are so wise," he would say, "Do you know everything?" "No, little man, the only one who knows everything is a fool." "More!" he would say. "All right, three more things, and then I must catch my breath: first—'If you don't stand for something, you will fall for something.' Second— 'The person who rides a donkey cannot avoid smelling its farts.' And finally— 'You may outrun what is running after you, but never what is running inside of you.'"

(Brussels airport. KATE *sits with their carry-on luggage.* RAYMOND *enters.)*

RAYMOND: Unbelievable. It's actually on time. Are you all right?

KATE: Just catching my breath. That turbulence was—a little challenging.

RAYMOND: You are doing great.

KATE: I was trying to imagine losing my entire family.

RAYMOND: Including cousins, I have counted forty three.

KATE: Forty three? Raymond. That's—Forty three?

RAYMOND: But at least I know their stories.

KATE: Just not the one that you were closest to.

RAYMOND: Felicien? We are more than close. We are overlapping. I cannot rest until I find him.

KATE: You never finished your story about you and Alphonse—you'd make a frame against a wall—

RAYMOND: Against a building, with eucalyptus wood. The walls were dried papyrus and metal for the roof. And Alphonse would make a deal for the power.

(A young ALPHONSE *appears.)*

ALPHONSE: All right—we can run the cord through his back window—and pay him after for electricity.

RAYMOND: So, two films a day…

ALPHONSE: Two? Why not three?

RAYMOND: And what—two hundred people?

ALPHONSE: No. Two twenty five, at least. Maybe two fifty.

RAYMOND: Fine.

ALPHONSE: And at ten cents apiece?

RAYMOND: My brother, we are in the film business!

ALPHONSE: Lucas and Spielberg! *(He disappears.)*

RAYMOND: When I finally saw a film in a real theater? On the big screen? Projected? My god! It was—you know—unbelievable! I—I had no breath. It was—just— Sorry, I am feeling so much. I didn't want to leave.

KATE: What was it? The first film you saw that way?

RAYMOND: *Gone With The Wind.*

KATE: *(Beat)* I want you to have this.

RAYMOND: What? Alan's camera? Are you—

KATE: And these.

*(*KATE *pulls out a leather case.* RAYMOND *examines them.)*

RAYMOND: His lenses, Kate, his Cookes! You are not serious.

KATE: He talked about wanting a set of these on our first date.

RAYMOND: No, Kate, this is too much.

KATE: They're wasted on me.

RAYMOND: But you could sell them.

KATE: Tell your stories, Ray.

RAYMOND: One day, I will try to pay you back. *(Beat)* You called me Ray.

KATE: Did I? Guess he flew over.

RAYMOND: Kate, you are my sister.

KATE: Forty three, Raymond? How you do it? Look at me, and I only lost one.

RAYMOND: The one you spoke your soul to. If I lost my wife—I cannot imagine.

KATE: Your wife?

RAYMOND: I will be married soon. To Hope. Hope Nganji.

KATE: You didn't tell me.

RAYMOND: She is from Burundi.

KATE: Burundi. That's—

RAYMOND: Rwanda and Burundi. We are twins separated at birth.
North and South. Reflections of each other.

KATE: That close.

RAYMOND: Felicien says we are like brothers whose wives do not trust each other—always watching with one eye to see how does their family get along. We are always watching.

KATE: What do you do with all your loss?

RAYMOND: In Rwanda, we say that our ancestors are walking with us every step. For our children, we are trying to forgive. *(Pause)* We are trying. So, you are finally going to see my country. But Kate, there is one thing I must warn you.

KATE: Warn me? What?

RAYMOND: Once you have been to Rwanda—

KATE: Yes?

RAYMOND:—you will always be coming back. It is the most beautiful place in the world.

(A sudden loud flight announcement. As they run off, the scream of jet engines crossfades with jungle sounds. Lights reveal a Huck Finn-style raft with DALLAIRE, *the* BOY, *and* MARK TWAIN, *who smokes a cigar as he walks back and forth with a long pole, moving them along.)*

DALLAIRE: So, where are we?

MARK TWAIN: Penetratin' the Interior, general. Never been up this river before, but we'll just forge ahead! I've found, the combination of ignorance and confidence is the surest guarantee of success.

DALLAIRE: Where are you taking us?

MARK TWAIN: Sit back and relax, sir. I'll get you there safely. Not familiar with this particular tributary, but no matter—they all seem to end up the same place. *(Pulls a book out of his coat)* Joe Conrad's no help. Plenty of metaphors, but not a single goddamned landmark!

DALLAIRE: I don't want to go back.

MARK TWAIN: Well, I don't want to be dead, but at least you have a choice in the matter.

DALLAIRE: Just let me rest.

MARK TWAIN: Oh, you will, sir, that's a given. Our demise is inevitable.

DALLAIRE: Can't be soon enough.

MARK TWAIN: That's the spirit! Beat a hasty retreat to the land of milk and boredom.

DALLAIRE: Well, I'd take that over—

MARK TWAIN: Find yourself a comfortable perch from which to watch the world go by. Knowing you could have made a difference.

DALLAIRE: I tried. And failed.

MARK TWAIN: Who hasn't? But you endured. By Seneca's definition a hero; "one who faces adversity and endures".

DALLAIRE: So—

MARK TWAIN: Just one last time, sir. Part of review requirements. I'm here to test your resolve.

DALLAIRE: How long—can't we at least fly?

MARK TWAIN: Funny you should ask. One of the Archangels was offering instruction—elementary levitation. But me—I choose to take the lessons of Icarus to heart. No sir, put me on the river any day! It's in the bones and blood!

(Blackout. A flash of lightning, followed by a loud clap of thunder and the sound of heavy rain. KATE and RAYMOND run in.)

KATE: Oh. My. God! I'm soaked.

RAYMOND: Welcome to Rwanda.

KATE: This is normal?

RAYMOND: Itumba. The rainy season.

KATE: How long does it normally last?

RAYMOND: Sometimes fifteen, twenty minutes. Sometimes hours.

KATE: So, what do you do?

RAYMOND: We stop. What choice do we have? We take a breath together.

KATE: Reminded Alan of New Orleans.

RAYMOND: A blessing.

KATE: From Imana.

RAYMOND: Imana, yes. It is a cleansing.

KATE: You really can smell the wood fires. Even in the rain.

RAYMOND: You saw the soapstone statue? The gorilla?

KATE: 'Digit,' you said? From "Gorillas in the Mist?"

RAYMOND: Rwanda's only movie star.

KATE: And this is the airport—

RAYMOND: His plane came over those hills.

KATE: It's sort of like "Who shot J F K?"

RAYMOND: Was it the French? The Belgians? R P F? Or maybe his wife? It never ends.

KATE: Maybe Bono! That would explain his dark glasses.

RAYMOND: *(Beat)* In '94, this rain, you know, brought miracles.

KATE: During the genocide?

RAYMOND: "The miracles of the rain." Many people have told me. How every day it would bring a pause in the killing.

KATE: That was the miracle?

RAYMOND: No, it was—when they cut people down at the roadblocks, often they would just hack a few times

and leave them to bleed out. But when the rain would
come, and the killers ran for shelter, sometimes the
drops would kiss the eyes of their victims, piled on the
side of the road. And bless the life back into them. That
was the miracle. The dead would awaken, sit up, then
rise to their feet and slowly walk away.

KATE: To where?

RAYMOND: To home, I guess. Or hospital. I was told
about one woman, she walked to her sister's house—
three kilometers.

KATE: Is she still alive?

RAYMOND: In a way. But she no longer speaks. Her
sister, though, is not.

KATE: *(Looking at the sky)* Two hours, huh?

RAYMOND: Or sometimes less.

(A clap of thunder)

(FELICIEN on his hill)

FELICIEN: For centuries, these hills kept out diseases—
and enemies from outside who could harm us. This is
why we are so many.
Who would not want to live in Rwanda? But our
children have children and their children, too. So, there
is sometimes the fear there will not be the room for us
all.

RAYMOND: *(To KATE)* So, the morning after he meets
Cat-reen, Thomas flies out to Egypt. Official business.
But she is all he can think about.

(THOMAS looks out.)

THOMAS: I ache. I ache for her.

RAYMOND: When he returns, they date for several
weeks, then finally she agrees to go with him for a
weekend at Lake Kivu—the Hotel Meridien.

THOMAS: Bunyanyezi!

CAT-REEN: I had to pee.

THOMAS: You stopped right—

CAT-REEN: We finished the whole bottle.

THOMAS: You could have peed in the lake.

CAT-REEN: Was that why you were smiling?

THOMAS: You are why I'm smiling.

(CAT-REEN *and* THOMAS *kiss.*)

CAT-REEN: Where's the page.

THOMAS: Here.
"Trying to give, I see that I have nothing."

CAT-REEN: "Trying to give, I see that I have nothing,
Seeing that I have nothing, I try to give myself,
Trying to give myself, I see that I am nothing,
Seeing that I am nothing, I desire to become,
Desiring to become, I live."

THOMAS: Mmm. "Desiring to become, I live."
Here's one:
"Philosophy teaches how man thinks he thinks; but
drinking shows how he really thinks." Do you see I
have fallen in love with you.

CAT-REEN: After so much wine, this must be how you
really think.

THOMAS: Cat-reen.

CAT-REEN: I love the way you say my name.

THOMAS: Cat-reen. You never told me about your
father.

CAT-REEN: An engineer. Very smart. He was a kind
man.

THOMAS: Was?

CAT-REEN: They found him in a ditch. Saddest day of my life.

THOMAS: I will find out who—

CAT-REEN: Almost twenty years ago. One of Rwanda's hard times.

THOMAS: I would do anything to keep you safe.

CAT-REEN: One day we will have a world beyond these troubles. No more Hutu and Tutsi. Only Hutsi.

(Lights on KATE *and* RAYMOND*)*

RAYMOND: Back in Kigali, her apartment, near Amahoro Stadium, can get very hot. The only ventilation comes from the crenellated cinder block wall.

(The stage goes black.)

THOMAS: Why are you laughing?

CAT-REEN: The electricity.

THOMAS: This is not funny.

CAT-REEN: Why did you do that?

THOMAS: Why can't you just plug something into the wall in this country?!

CAT-REEN: I never asked for an air conditioner.

THOMAS: You ought to be able to— This is ridiculous.

CAT-REEN: Oh my god! Thomas, look! The lights are out in the entire neighborhood!

THOMAS: Stop laughing!

CAT-REEN: They are going to kill me! *(She lights a candle.)*

THOMAS: I'm the one who did it.

CAT-REEN: You're right. I'll tell them. Hey, everyone— he's up here!

(THOMAS *blows out the candle.*)

THOMAS: I prefer the dark.

CAT-REEN: Oh, wait! What are you doing? That's—

THOMAS: Do you?

CAT-REEN: That's—Oh Thomas, be careful. Your fingers—

THOMAS: Yes?

CAT-REEN: A little higher.

(*Lights find* RAYMOND.)

RAYMOND: (*To* KATE) And the Hutu government hated Tutsi women. Even more than men. One could write whole books about why. Back in Paris, Thomas and his wife, Paulette, enjoy a comfortable family life. But the way he feels with Cat-reen—

THOMAS: —my Bunyanyezi! What could I do?

(FELICIEN *returns to his story.*)

FELICIEN: When I was young, the Belgian administrators gave us cards which we must carry. Another story I must tell. Cards with photos that say if you are Tutsi or Hutu or Twa. Which divided us sharply. Before these cards—to be Tutsi or Hutu means only if you are doing well or not, but always it can change. If a man worked hard or married well, with 10 cows or more, a Hutu could become Tutsi. But our cards would no longer allow this. It stole away the dreams of many Hutu and brought darkness to their eyes. But we all know each other on these hills. From forever. And everyone knows Felicien. I tell them stories.

BAGASORA: (*O S*) Sibomana! (*He appears with a glass of scotch.*)

THOMAS: Colonel Bagasora!

BAGASORA: I didn't know you were back, Mister Radio. Mister Smooth Voice.

THOMAS: That's me. I'm in for meetings.

BAGASORA: Mister President's Hutu History Boy.

THOMAS: Yes. You listen to my show?

BAGASORA: What a life you lead! If I were you? I would be at home in Paris right now, eating a big, thick, juicy filet mignon at some fancy restaurant, Mister First-Class Passenger.

THOMAS: Every day I am grateful for such a good assignment.

BAGASORA: Well, you have married well. How is Paulette?

THOMAS: She is fine, thank you. So is Chantal. I will be back with them soon. And your wife?

BAGASORA: You know the old saying: "The Tutsi, you lodge him in the corner and he forces you out of the house?"

THOMAS: There are many versions: "The Tutsi, you lodge him in the lobby and he intrudes on you in bed."

BAGASORA: Yes. So many ways they can sneak into our house.

THOMAS: Of course, we must be vigilant.

BAGASORA: I hear, though, there are still Hutu among us who are "open-minded." Who still cannot resist—a certain taste. They must be made aware that if it came to light—their minds might be opened even further.

THOMAS: Do we have any names?

BAGASORA: None that are confirmed.

THOMAS: I will look into it, of course. We cannot be too careful.

BAGASORA: Exactly. On your next trip, Thomas, you must bring me a bottle of Crown Royal from the duty-free. And some of that fancy after-shave. My wife loves it!

THOMAS: I'll make a note.

BAGASORA: Rwanda for the Hutu!

THOMAS: Rwanda for the Hutu!

RAYMOND: He writes about a dinner party at which Bagasora—with General Dallaire sitting right across from him—comes right out and says:

BAGASORA: We will exterminate them from the earth!

(BAGASORA and THOMAS and BAGASORA look at each other, as CAT-REEN re-appears.)

CAT-REEN: Thomas! Thank god you are here. My mother called. There's been a massacre in the Bugasera. Thomas, four hundred people! All Tutsi. Women, children, one of my cousins and his wife. You must do something.

THOMAS: Four hundred? Are you sure? I will look into it, of course.

CAT-REEN: You must find out who is responsible. You know who to ask. Promise me you will.

THOMAS: Of course, my love. We cannot stand for this.

CAT-REEN: Oh, Thomas. If only the world had more good men like you.

(Pause)

THOMAS: Cat-reen?

CAT-REEN: Yes, my sweet Thomas?

THOMAS: I will never let anything happen to you.

(Lights change.)

RAYMOND: From that moment, Thomas goes out of his way to publicly agree with everything the President says against the Tutsi.

THOMAS: *(On the air)* The Hutu must be careful and be ready. The tall grass must be cleared. The only solution. Rwanda for the Hutu!

RAYMOND: In this way, he believes he can buy safety for Cat-reen. This is his deal with the Devil.

THOMAS: Any man who does not choose love first is not a man!

(Flowers stretch out to the horizon. Smoking volcanoes loom in the distance. FELICIEN speaks from his hill.)

FELICIEN: For all their beauty, once they are harvested, dried and ground into powder, these flowers are powerful poison.
Fortunately, only to insects. "Pyrethrum" they are called. Our third largest export. Only tea and coffee do we have more of. These flowers can solve the problem of infestation.

(Movement among the stalks. DALLAIRE sits up and looks around. MARK TWAIN appears in a tree above.)

DALLAIRE: I know just where we are. Virunga. So, I'm back.

MARK TWAIN: And thanks to pharmaceuticals, you got here four months before you arrived.

DALLAIRE: Why here? Why show me this?

MARK TWAIN: Little glimpse of what you were walking into.

(A group of young men sing a popular Interahamwe song, as they train together in the field beyond. We only see their trainer, who demonstrates on a roughly-made dummy. A FRENCH PARATROOPER smokes as he watches.)

PRESIDENTIAL GUARD: Head here. Neck here. Organs here. Spine. Groin cut. And back of the knees. Or— Now watch carefully! —here is the Achilles tendon. It is your friend. It buys you time. If you do not have time to finish the job, you can cut here, and they are going nowhere. So when you come back later, they will be waiting for you, you will see. Again! Head here. Neck here. Organs here. Spine. Groin cut. Back of the knees. Achilles tendon. Now—everyone mark these targets with your partner!

MARK TWAIN: Every commune, every hillside, every able-bodied man. The charm's wound up.

DALLAIRE: I told New York.

MARK TWAIN: They didn't care.

DALLAIRE: They wanted simple.

MARK TWAIN: Amen and hallelujah!

(The BOY *pokes up out of the pyrethrum with a stick and watches them train.)*

PRESIDENTIAL GUARD: *(Sharp burst of a whistle)* Wait, wait! What is that, you dumb country Hutu!? Why am I wasting my time here? Is that what I showed you? No. You must listen to me! I said, "Your blow must be clean and—what?—decisive." *(To the group)* "Clean and decisive." You must know where the artery is. *(Back to the one)* Where is the artery in your neck? Yes? So why are you cutting over here? *(To the group)* You must be—what?

TEENAGE BOYS' VOICES: *(In unison)* Clean and decisive!

PRESIDENTIAL GUARD: Clean. *(Thud)* And. *(Thud)* Decisive. *(Thud)* Otherwise, you will be hacking away all day!

(Laughter from the group)

(The BOY *mimics them.)*

PRESIDENTIAL GUARD: Stop cutting like women!!!
You are men! You are Hutu! You are proud!
This is hard work. You will need all your energy!
Rwanda is counting on you for self-defense to keep her
 free!
Now, the president wants us to make lists of all the
Tutsi where you live.
You know who is living around you.
 who is living on your hill.
 who can be trusted.
Together, we must keep a careful eye.
Now, go home and remember what I am telling you!
And then, tomorrow? —we will learn to use grenades!

(Enthusiastic response)

PRESIDENTIAL GUARD: *Interahamwe!!!*
We work together, we fight together, we win together!

(Another whistle burst)

BOYS: *(Voices in unison)*
Work together, fight together, win together!

(The trainer blows his whistle.)

BOYS: Work together, fight together, win together!

(The trainer blows his whistle)

BOYS: Work together, fight together, win together!

(The sound of forty or fifty whistles blowing at once)

*(The BOYS picks up their chant. As they begin singing, a few
keep time with their whistles. The sound of trucks, loading,
then receding into the distance, taking most of the boys
home. ALPHONSE enters from the training ground, walking
across the field. INNOCENT, a little older, enters carrying a
machete.)*

INNOCENT: Hey, little brother!

(ALPHONSE ignores INNOCENT.)

INNOCENT: Hey, you dumb Hutu!

ALPHONSE: Shut up.

INNOCENT: What is the matter? Why are you walking home?

ALPHONSE: I prefer to walk.

INNOCENT: Me, too. We can walk together.

ALPHONSE: Suit yourself.

INNOCENT: You must be strong.

ALPHONSE: I'm not good at this.

INNOCENT: That is why we practice, little brother.

ALPHONSE: I'm not your little brother.

INNOCENT: What is your name?

ALPHONSE: Alphonse.

INNOCENT: You are worrying too much, Alphonse.

ALPHONSE: I am not a soldier.

INNOCENT: Why—because he picks you out? You will learn.

ALPHONSE: I know where to cut.

INNOCENT: It is not enough to know where, you must know why! You need to use your heart. You must hate them.

ALPHONSE: I am hating the R P F, but...

INNOCENT: Hutu, wake up! You are one of us. They are coming to enslave us. Feel your power! Hutu power!

ALPHONSE: But my neighbors do not hurt me.

INNOCENT: Maybe not yet.

ALPHONSE: Why do we need to kill them? Why not drive them all away?

INNOCENT: Don't you listen to the radio? We drove
them out in '59 and now they're back, banging at our
door. This time we need to finish the job! We will all
help each other. You will learn.

ALPHONSE: I've never seen you before. Why are you
here?

INNOCENT: I am Innocent. Innocent Sembagaye. I am
here to visit my aunt. She has been sick. My cousin,
Mateus, lives there on your hill.

ALPHONSE: Oh, Mateus! He is great. You are the one he
was telling me about. From Burundi.

INNOCENT: I was. Now I am living here. In the south.
They are training us there also.

ALPHONSE: He told me about your family. The radio
said the Tutsi Government killed many Hutu in
Burundi.

INNOCENT: Many thousands. I lost my father, my
little brother, and four of my sisters. Soon after, my
mother—Mateus' aunt—she died of grief.

(A long moment of silence)

ALPHONSE: So you came here to Rwanda?

INNOCENT: To be free. Now I live in a refugee camp—
with nowhere to grow food for my children. Still, I am
free. But before I left, I answered what they did to me.
That is when I learned what I capable of.

ALPHONSE: You mean you killed someone?

INNOCENT: I took his family. All of them. I know it
sounds impossible, but you only need to start.
The first cut is the hardest. And I will tell you this—
you must not look into their eyes. These snakes are
crafty. They will soften your arm and weaken your
resolve. We need each other to be strong. Remember

what they have done to us. Are you with us? Can I count on you, Alphonse?

ALPHONSE: Yes. Yes, of course.

INNOCENT: You're not a Tutsi lover, are you? Icyitso?

ALPHONSE: Fuck you! No!! I will be a great fighter— you will see!

INNOCENT: I know. And we will make each other stronger. We work together! We fight together!

ALPHONSE & INNOCENT: We win together!

INNOCENT: I will see you at work, my Hutu Brother!

(ALPHONSE *watches as* INNOCENT *leaves.* DALLAIRE *takes his head in his hands. Somewhere above him,* MARK TWAIN *re-appears, still smoking his cigar.*)

MARK TWAIN: I was born at a rare juncture of time and space when Halley's Comet was visible from earth as it passed by, and, according to some rather well-informed sources, it occurred next again on the day that I died. I take comfort in that heavenly symmetry; it offers persuasive evidence that for all our delusions of progress, we're actually just movin' in circles.

(BAGASORA *appears.*)

DALLAIRE: So, am I here or not?

MARK TWAIN: Well, there's a cry for the Ages.

DALLAIRE: Heaven must want me to stop him! Why can't he see me?!

MARK TWAIN: 'Fraid we're just here to observe. Bit of a preview of eternal rest. How it'll feel.

DALLAIRE: Can't you do something?! Aren't you an angel?

MARK TWAIN: Not even remotely. More of a passing reflection.

DALLAIRE: I could do it now. My duty to stop him.

MARK TWAIN: A man performs but one duty in his life—the duty of contenting his spirit. Of making himself agreeable to himself.

(DALLAIRE *pulls out his revolver.*)

DALLAIRE: Right here, you bastard!

MARK TWAIN: So, part of you still wants to save the world.

DALLAIRE: Dear God, a single bullet in his butcher's brain!!

(BAGASORA *speaks to unseen masses.*)

BAGASORA: The Hutu Ten Commandments.

(THOMAS *enters* CAT-REEN's *apartment.*)

THOMAS: Cat-reen? Cat-reen, I have been missing you—where are you?

BAGASORA: 1) Every Hutu must know that the Tutsi woman, wherever she may be, is working for the Tutsi ethnic cause.

CAT-REEN: You can take your air conditioner. Take all your books!

THOMAS: What are you saying?

CAT-REEN: This is no place for you. You live in Paris.

BAGASORA: In consequence, any Hutu is a traitor who:
—Acquires a Tutsi wife;
—Acquires a Tutsi concubine;
—Acquires a Tutsi secretary or protégée.

THOMAS: Why would you talk like this? Please—what has happened?

CAT-REEN: The things you said. You think I don't have ears?

THOMAS: Oh no! Cat-reen, I told you not to listen! Forgive me, please. Those things—that is not me. You know me—I could never. It is a game. That I must play, avoiding all suspicion. Forgive me—I would rather die than have you hate me. But they must never think— They're not my words!

CAT-REEN: But people trust your words. They will believe you.

THOMAS: To keep you safe, Cat-reen. It is all for you!

CAT-REEN: Dear god, I hate this world. Thomas, I do. Where we believe one thing but say another? The things you said—This world is not for me.

BAGASORA: 2) Hutu must know that our Hutu daughters are more worthy and more conscientious as women, as wives and as mothers.

THOMAS: I hate myself for ever saying that.

CAT-REEN: My sweet Thomas, I knew this was not you.

THOMAS: It has to stop. Cat-reen, I need to hold you. Forgive me, please.

THOMAS: GugNo, I bought you something.

CAT-REEN: I told you, no, you are enough for me.

THOMAS: I couldn't help myself. The moment when I saw this, it was meant for only you.

CAT-REEN: You like to drive me crazy.

THOMAS: Yes, I do.

BAGASORA: 4) All Hutu must know that all Tutsi are dishonest in business. Their only goal is ethnic superiority.

CAT-REEN: I got you something, too—your favorite— Guinness.

THOMAS: Mmm. You know what that does to me.

CAT-REEN: All right then, what did you get?

THOMAS: Now, where did I put it?

CAT-REEN: Sibomana!

THOMAS: Bunyanyezi!

(THOMAS *hands* CAT-REEN *a fancy French box. She opens it and pulls out a beautiful, very distinctive dress.*)

THOMAS: Do you like it?

CAT-REEN: Oh Thomas! I love it! It's beautiful!

THOMAS: I cannot imagine my life without you.

(CAT-REEN *and* THOMAS *kiss.*)

CAT-REEN: Thomas Sibomana, we were meant to be together. Now let me take my shower, so I can come back to you.

(CAT-REEN *goes into the bathroom.* THOMAS *looks out.*)

THOMAS: I am not a racist. Cat-reen was my soulmate, Tutsi or not. I cared deeply for Paulette, but if there was only one, it was Cat-reen. In a perverse way, I even had an interest in the conflict getting worse. Because the worse it got, the more sense it made to keep our relationship secret.

BAGASORA: 8) Hutu must stop taking pity on the Tutsi.

THOMAS: Haby has started having Tutsi women arrested.

CAT-REEN: *(Off)* It is his wife, I am sure. She resents us.

(CAT-REEN *enters in her new dress.* THOMAS *pulls out a Polaroid camera, takes a photo of her, then fans it in the air.*)

CAT-REEN: Do you like it?

(THOMAS *nods.*)

CAT-REEN: Then, take it off me and come to bed.

BAGASORA: 9) Hutu, wherever they be, must stand united,—

THOMAS: I can't.

CAT-REEN: Is something wrong?

BAGASORA; —in solidarity, firm and vigilant—

THOMAS: I'm all in knots. They have asked me to do things.

CAT-REEN: What, Thomas? What things? What sort of things?

BAGASORA: —against their common enemy: the Tutsi!

CAT-REEN: Tell me. Am I your Cat-reen?

THOMAS: Of course. You are my life.

CAT-REEN: Your other life.

THOMAS: No, this. Here. In this room—this is my life. My public life—I am wanting it more and more to be done. I cannot be myself and keep doing this job.

CAT-REEN: I know what a good heart beats in you.

THOMAS: A troubled heart.

CAT-REEN: But why?

THOMAS: The killings you heard about. Your cousin, his wife. They are only practicing. Preparing to kill more.

BAGASORA: 10) The Hutu Ideology must be taught to Hutu of every age, spreading the word wherever he goes. Rwanda for the Hutu! *(He disappears.)*

CAT-REEN: Thomas—tell me!

THOMAS: A nun, an Italian nun called in to Radio France International. And on the air, she told them she had solid proof that Hutu politicians—not just peasants—were the ones responsible.

(Pause)

CAT-REEN: Don't tell me—

THOMAS: They were there the moment she hung up.

CAT-REEN: Oh no, Thomas. My god. A nun?

THOMAS: They wanted me to call up and denounce her—to deny it. To lie and say she's a spy for the R P F. But I refused. I had to draw the line. It's all too much.

CAT-REEN: I am so proud of you! Who are these people?! What will happen to us? And to our beautiful Rwanda?

THOMAS: Let me take you far away. It is too dangerous here.

CAT-REEN: No, Thomas, this is where I live. This is my home. I am from Rwanda. Come let me hear you breathe next to my ear.

(*Lights shift.*)

THOMAS: I had refused, but only by pretending to be sick, to have lost my voice. I couldn't tell her that. I hated that I was not the man she believed I was. We made love. Then talked again about a different Rwanda. That might be coming. A Rwanda of 'Hutsi.'

(ALPHONSE *enters, carrying a machete, on his way somewhere.* DALLAIRE *follows, invisible to all, and watches.*)

RAYMOND: *(O S)* Alphonse!

(ALPHONSE *keeps walking, as* RAYMOND *runs in, with a fishing line.*)

RAYMOND: Hey! Where are you going? Why don't you answer me?

ALPHONSE: *(Looking behind him)* What do you want?

RAYMOND: I am flying back to New York next week. I have missed you, my little brother. Come on—the fish are jumping!

ALPHONSE: Not today.

RAYMOND: Not today? I have to tell you about New York. About what I'm learning.

ALPHONSE: I'm busy.

RAYMOND: I came to find you yesterday. Where have you been?

ALPHONSE: Leave me alone.

RAYMOND: Oh, you are funny, Hutu boy! Hey, this is me—it's Raymond!

ALPHONSE: This is not a good time.

RAYMOND: Why not? Who are you going off to see?

ALPHONSE: Mateus.

RAYMOND: Mateus? When did you start to spend time with him? I am missing you, little brother.

ALPHONSE: I'm not your brother.

RAYMOND: More than my own brother, yes you are—like it or not.

ALPHONSE: I don't like it anymore. Now go away.

RAYMOND: You are crazy. Why are you—I'm leaving soon.

ALPHONSE: *(Sees someone coming)* Then leave! Things are different here now. I cannot be seen with you.

RAYMOND: I think you are taking the radio too seriously. Alphonse! Don't walk away from me. Alphonse. This is not you.

INNOCENT enters, nodding to ALPHONSE as he passes, and sizes up RAYMOND.

(ALPHONSE *hurries off after him, leaving* RAYMOND *in disbelief. He shakes his head, then climbs up to* FELICIEN *on his hill.)*

FELICIEN: *Agasozi kagufi kagushyikiriza akarekare.*
Climbing even a short hill will bring us to a higher
point. Why are you sad?

RAYMOND: I am only concentrating.

FELICIEN: Then tell me, do you remember the story of
Gihanga?

RAYMOND: Gihanga? Of course.

FELICIEN: King Nyamigezi had three cousins who were
great seers.

RAYMOND: The Ubukara.

FELICIEN: My grandson is a clever boy. Do you
remember their names?

RAYMOND: Gakara, Gacu, and Ka…Kazi…

FELICIEN: Kazigaaba. The greatest seers the kingdom
had ever known. But many just laughed at their
dreams, would not take their advice. The gift of vision,
Raymond, is a powerful thing. To those who don't
wish to consider the future, sometimes we see too
much.

RAYMOND: Felicien, I need to travel, so I can look back
at our world from far away. And only then, I think, can
I know what life for me is meant to be.

FELICIEN: You will come back to tell our stories with
your camera.

RAYMOND: It is not easy for me to leave you.

FELICIEN: Physical distance is not our measure. Not for
us—we are always connected.

(CAT-REEN's *apartment.* THOMAS *enters with a*
MacDonald's bag and bottle of Fanta.)

THOMAS: Happy American Fourth of July!

CAT-REEN: I could hear the fireworks.

THOMAS: MacDonald's. They flew it in from Brussels.

CAT-REEN: So, your guest of honor? With three names?
Did she come?

THOMAS: Sandra Day O'Connor? She was there. The
international symbol of justice. Here in our little
Rwanda. I have never seen Haby so nervous. So soon
after that slaughter in Bugasera.

CAT-REEN: So, what did she say?

THOMAS: We were standing there. Yellow wrappers
littering the lawn. Just waiting for her to point her
righteous finger. Putting us all on notice for Human
Rights violations. And they're serving us hamburger.
The irony was a meal in itself. Big Mac?

CAT-REEN: So, tell me!

THOMAS: She talked about the court system in America.
Her French is atrocious, by the way. And what we
could learn from them.

CAT-REEN: What else?

THOMAS: "But this," she says, "is not the main point of
my trip." I can see Haby is dying.

CAT-REEN: So, what did she say?

THOMAS: She is very concerned about what she is
hearing, she says. It is time for this business to end.

CAT-REEN: Finally, someone.

THOMAS: She will bring the world's attention—

CAT-REEN: Someone is watching.

THOMAS: Dedicating herself—

CAT-REEN: Amazing woman!

THOMAS: —to the plight of our mountain gorillas. They
must be saved!

CAT-REEN: Oh no, Thomas. No, please.

THOMAS: As for the killing. I don't think she even knows.

CAT-REEN: Of course not.

THOMAS: And her trip? Was sponsored by the U S Information Agency!

CAT-REEN: They won't protect us. No one will.

THOMAS: So, Haby smiles at the Ambassador as he finishes his burger, and we all watch fireworks. And our National Band plays an off-key, hip-hop version of the Star Spangled Banner. Completely surreal.

CAT-REEN: And so is this. *(She holds up a newspaper.)*

THOMAS: Kangura? Why did you get this? Kangura is trash. These cartoons? They hate all Tutsi women. Why would you want this?

CAT-REEN: To know my enemies. Those who would kill me. How they think. Thomas...what's going to happen?

(The sun is setting on FELICIEN's *hill.)*

FELICIEN: Then Lucifer made up his mind: he would
Rebel against the Lord. He sought a place
In space that would be suitable for war.
He had a vague presentiment that God
Might be like that innocent looking sheep
Which suddenly became a thundercloud.
The rebel Lucifer began, by God's
Command, to shrivel, but he did not die.

*(*MARK TWAIN *in a separate light.)*

MARK TWAIN: Most people are bothered by those passages of Scripture they do not understand, but the passages that bother me are those I do understand.

(From here to the end of the ACT, FELICIEN *is lit by the light of a fire he is tending on his hill.)*

(In CAT-REEN*'S apartment, the light of a television bounces on* THOMAS*'s face, as he drinks a Guiness.)*

CAT-REEN: So, what did you tell the President?

THOMAS: That I was sick. I couldn't fly.

CAT-REEN: And you don't think—?

THOMAS: Bunyanyezi, it's fine. I wanted to be here with you—not at another boring meeting in Dar Es Salaam.

CAT-REEN: With me, you mean, and your child.

THOMAS: My what?

CAT-REEN: Your child.

THOMAS: You mean—?

CAT-REEN: He will be here in September.

THOMAS: You're serious? This completely—

CAT-REEN: Are you angry?

THOMAS: Angry? No, I'm trying to, what—my life— this just throws everything— But no. A child? I'm— No, Cat-reen, with you I think I'm ready! We'll have to plan, of course. You said September?

CAT-REEN: Our first little Hutsi.

THOMAS: I am upside down and inside out. The world, Cat-reen, the world is about to change.

(The sound of East African drums, which progressively build through the end of the act. We see the BOY *playing with sticks.)*

(Lights on KATE *and* RAYMOND. *They are looking at one of* ALAN*'s notebooks.)*

KATE: Three and a half years?

RAYMOND: Preparing for it, yes. Though, of course, it really started in '59.

KATE: And the massacre Cat-reen was talking about?

RAYMOND: Testing. To see who would protest. And once they saw it was safe, Alphonse said they even announced it on the radio.

D J: Attention, Kigali, attention! In the next few days, something very big will happen.

(FELICIEN *appears in the golden late-day light on his hill.*)

RAYMOND: This is amazing. Alan completely reconstructed it. Eyewitnesses on both sides, historical facts, things I never knew. Like music.

KATE: So, good—we let him guide us. Find the rhythm and let it build. Where does he start?

RAYMOND: "Habyarimana boards his plane in Dar Es Salaam."

KATE: *(Begins taking notes)* Can we maybe get news footage of that?

RAYMOND: "April 6, 1994. Around 7 P M. President Habyarimana boards his Mystère Falcon jet—a gift from the French Government—and heads home from a summit of African leaders, about an hour and a half flight away."

KATE: Keep going.

RAYMOND: "They've pressured him to stop delaying and implement the peace treaty."

KATE: Good. Okay. Then, we start introducing witnesses.

(*One by one, faces are lit.*)

BAGASORA: Peace? This treaty is a joke! Thirty years of freedom from the Tutsi, and now he lets them back? He is giving Rwanda away!

(*The sound of a soccer game on T V adds to the mix.*)

DALLAIRE: I'm switching back and forth between
C N N and the Africa Cup on television. One of the
few luxuries we enjoy.

(The BOY *has made a plane out of sticks and begins to fly it
around.)*

RAYMOND: "As part of the treaty agreement, General
Dallaire and his UNAMIR troops have escorted
six hundred R P F soldiers, their commanders and
politicians through huge crowds in Kigali."

R P F SOLDIER: All my life, from Uganda, we have
looked to these hills. The hills of Rwanda. The home of
our ancestors.

DALLAIRE: Operation Clean Corridor.

BAGASORA: Idiots!

R P F SOLDIER: All our lives, we have waited for this.

RAYMOND: "They've been given a position up on a hill
in the Parliament building."

BAGASORA: Letting them in—that's bad enough—but
then he puts them above us on a hill? Habyarimana is
an idiot!!

R P F SOLDIER: They say there is no longer room for us
here in Rwanda. But here we are!

BAGASORA: Power-sharing is death. Today, we smile
and shake their hand. Tomorrow, we will cut it off.

RAYMOND: Then, we hear the plane.

(The sound of the executive jet.)

KATE: Got it.

RAYMOND: "As the light drains from the sky, the
president's plane appears on the horizon. Suddenly, an
unusual announcement on R T L M:" Cut to:

D J: Attention, Kigali. Attention. The President's jet is
approaching the airport.

RAYMOND: "The French co-pilot's daughter, Sylvie Minaberry, tunes in to the plane's radio frequency, as her father arrives home—a family ritual."

KATE: The co-pilot's daughter? Where'd he find that?

RAYMOND: Says here, from a lawsuit. She is suing the French government.

KATE: Suing? For what?

RAYMOND: "To find out the truth about what her father was doing in Rwanda."

KATE: Unbelievable. Keep going.

(We hear an airplane radio transmission in French.)

RAYMOND: "She hears something she's never heard before; the control tower asks if the Presidents are on board."

INNOCENT: The new Hutu President of Burundi, Cyprien Nsabimana, is getting a ride back home.

RAYMOND: "They ask five times."

INNOCENT: Enjoying Rwandan hospitality.

THOMAS: Burundi; our evil twin reflected in a funhouse mirror.

RAYMOND: "She hears the pilot's pissed-off voice say:"

FRENCH PILOT: *(In French)* Who is this? No—there's nobody on the plane. *(In English)* What the fuck?

THOMAS: Haby's exhausted. Ready to roll over. The peace accords have made him obsolete.

ALAN: There were eight other passengers. People seem to forget.

KATE: We can cut in names, faces.

RAYMOND: "In the airport V I P lounge, the director of the office of the president is waiting for him with papers to sign—"

ALAN: Eight human beings.

RAYMOND: "—to officially end the political logjam which has paralyzed the peace process."

THOMAS: If not for my hunger to be with Cat-reen, I would have been up there, too.

RAYMOND: "But, as the plane prepares for landing, suddenly, the runway lights go out."

FRENCH PILOT: *(In French)* Holy shit!

RAYMOND: "The pilot pulls the plane up hard and circles back around for a second approach, passing directly over the President's residence."

PRESIDENTIAL GUARD: The Presidential Guard is the government's first line of defense. We are the Secret Service, the Navy Seals.

JEAN/R P F SOLDIER: "Stay back, *inyenzi!*" they warn us.

PRESIDENTIAL GUARD: We have prepared the Hutu men of every region. And for every one, they have a list.

JEAN/R P F SOLDIER: "Or else when you arrive, there will be no-one left to govern."

PRESIDENTIAL GUARD: We are ready. We sleep with our guns by the bed.

JEAN/R P F SOLDIER: No more ceasefires, we tell them. No more games; our people are dying!

RAYMOND: "At R P F headquarters in Mulindi, a former tea plantation near Uganda, General Paul Kagame also watches The Africa Cup on his T V."

DALLAIRE: The semi-final. Mali versus Zambia.

THOMAS: Cat-reen's now watching, too.

DALLAIRE: Mali's behind—it's four to nothing.

CAT-REEN: This game is over.

THOMAS: Just playing out the clock.

FRENCH PILOT: *(In French)* Sylvie—I know you're listening—what's for dinner?

DALLAIRE: About to be eliminated.

RAYMOND: "A blinding flash of light from Masaka hill—"

KATE: Right.

RAYMOND: "—as someone with considerable training fires a Russian-made, surface-to-air missile—"

FRENCH PILOT: *(In French)* Hey—what was that?

RAYMOND: "A narrow miss."

THOMAS: The people I trust most suspect "Le Clan de Madame"—if not Madame herself.

ALPHONSE: After choir practice, Father Ntzanga tells us:

FRENCH PILOT: Jean-Pierre?

ALPHONSE: "All Good Christian Hutu must be ready, for what will be required."

INNOCENT: I will never go back to Burundi again. My only hope lives here.

R P F SOLDIER: On watch, it's strange. It's quiet, but there's something in the air.

INNOCENT: We must protect Rwanda—we must keep Rwanda free!

R P F SOLDIER: Like the quiet before a storm.

INNOCENT: Rwanda for the Hutu!!!

RAYMOND: "Another flash of light from the field—"

PRESIDENTIAL GUARD: In the barracks, we are laughing, listening to the radio.

RAYMOND: "But this one hits the mark."

The BOY runs downstage, pointing into the air.

R P F SOLDIER: Flares on the hill, an explosion—

PRESIDENTIAL GUARD: We grab our guns and race outside.

R P F SOLDIER: We are under attack!!

PRESIDENTIAL GUARD: Running in every direction.

R P F SOLDIER: Victory!! R P F!!!

RAYMOND: "The plane comes end-over-end, in a fireball out of the sky."

PRESIDENTIAL GUARD: We're yelling and pointing to the sky.

INNOCENT: Freedom!

MARK TWAIN: A pair of kings.

THOMAS: Two birds with one stone.

KATE: It's raining Hutu Presidents.

INNOCENT: Freedom!!

ALPHONSE: All good Christian Hutu.

PRESIDENTIAL GUARD: Hell! All hell is breaking loose!!

ALPHONSE: We must be ready.

INNOCENT: Freedom!!! I am ready! Just tell me what to do!!

PRESIDENTIAL GUARD: Get the list.

R P F SOLDIER: We taste it!

INNOCENT: The radio says it's time!

R P F SOLDIER: It's finally time!

D J: Now do your work!!

INNOCENT: Well, I say, "We are ready now! So, let the work begin!!"

(An explosion rocks the theatre, followed by a brilliant flash of light up in the air, then all sounds stop.)

RAYMOND: "And metal and bone rain down like seeds of death, sowing themselves deep in the President's garden."

(A sharp insistent knocking. CAT-REEN's apartment. THOMAS pulls out a revolver and nods to CAT-REEN.)

CAT-REEN: *Alo? Qu'es qu'il y a?*

MAN'S VOICE: *Un ami— Un ami de Thomas.*

(THOMAS motions CAT-REEN to step back.)

THOMAS: *Qu'es qu'il y a?*

MAN'S VOICE: *Thomas? Le president. Le president est mort.*

(Ambulance lights and squawking walkie-talkies, as two E M S workers rush a body on a gurney into a pool of light. DALLAIRE sits up and addresses the audience.)

DALLAIRE: When I first arrived in Kigali, I met an American analyst, who had been sent to assess the value of a U S involvement in Rwanda. But he said he was recommending against it— "There's nothing here!" he told them. "No oil, no diamonds, no strategic value—nothing! All that is here," he said, "is humans."

(The sound and time resume, as he lies back and is wheeled quickly away, and the first movement of Mozart's Requiem *begins to play.)*

RAYMOND: "The Presidential Guard begin to work their way through the wealthy neighborhood, house-to-house, checking off names from their lists, screams, gunshots. Drunken teenagers with pangas set up a roadblock. Smash cut to boots and rifles, R P F soldiers digging in, preparing for a fight. Then everything goes black, as the electricity goes out, and people huddle in their homes together, listening in the dark to their crackling transistor radios."

THOMAS: *(To* CAT-REEN*)* Doesn't open this door for anyone, do you hear? I will be back as soon as I can.

RAYMOND: "He gets in his car and heads for the airport. On the radio, his own R T L M already has the story. And the spin—pouring salt into the country's gaping wound:"

D J: The President's plane has been shot down by the Belgian U N soldiers, on behalf of the R P F Inyenzi.

THOMAS: I come to a military roadblock. Usually, my government car and I D will get me through quickly. But tonight, things are different. The soldier takes my I D and stares at it. For a very long time. Finally, he looks up at me, smiling, and says:

PRESIDENTIAL GUARD: "We'll soon know in this country—who deserves to live."

CAT-REEN: Then, even the radio goes off the air. So now there is only darkness—darkness and fear. When it finally returns, they tell us:

D J: "The President is dead. Stay in your homes. Stay where you are and remain calm."

CAT-REEN: And then, for the rest of the night, they play us music—classical music.

THOMAS: Mozart's Requiem in D Minor.

(Beat)

CAT-REEN: To keep us calm.

(The frenetic third movement of Mozart's Requiem fills the theatre. Blackout)

END OF ACT TWO

ACT THREE

(Music of Bach, mathematical and precise. Once its themes have been introduced, it begins to cross with tribal chant and singing that bring together East and West.)

(FELICIEN appears with his walking stick.)

FELICIEN: Once there was a monster who swallowed everything. Every day, the villagers brought food to him, huge quantities of food, though he was never satisfied. In desperation, they gathered together all the resources of the world and gave those to him. He ate them, as well. Still not satisfied, he devoured the earth, the sun, the moon, the stars but he was still hungry. Then, as nothing remained, neither in the heavens nor on the earth, he looked at his hand. He thought it huge, plump and appetizing. So, he ate one of his fingers, then two, then three, and so on. He crunched up his right hand, he crunched up his left hand, his arms, both his shoulders. But still he was hungry. And in the end—he consumed himself altogether.

(KATE and RAYMOND sit in a Kigali cafe. Their WAITER arrives, then shows them two bottles before carefully opening each in front of them and pouring. KATE watches, fascinated. The WAITER leaves.)

KATE: So, what is that about?

RAYMOND: It's a tradition in Rwanda, ever since the death of our last great Tutsi Mwami, our last king. To be safe.

KATE: You mean, he was poisoned?

RAYMOND: He went to Burundi to see a Belgian doctor who gave him shots that killed him.

KATE: On purpose?

RAYMOND: That is the story.

KATE: Leave town for treatment, given the wrong penicillin—sounds like a classic venereal disease story.

RAYMOND: You must not let people hear you say that here.

KATE: How long ago was that?

RAYMOND: It sparked the Hutu Revolution. 1959.

KATE: And that's why—

RAYMOND:—they open the bottle in front of you. Always.

KATE: You mean, "Don't worry, I didn't poison you"?

RAYMOND: Exactly.

KATE: That's comforting. (Beat) I can't stop thinking about your story—the miracles of the rain. Those people just waking up and walking away. Where did they go? And what's this?

She extends her hand for him to shake, then rests her other on her forearm.

RAYMOND: Another tradition. A sign of respect.

KATE: Is it respect? Or 'Don't worry, I'll keep my hands out where you can see 'em?'

RAYMOND: Perhaps in the beginning, yes, but—

KATE: I guess trust is not high on the list here. Hey—no poison, no weapons—let's be friends!

RAYMOND: You make me laugh. I enjoy to be with you.

KATE: So, when do you visit Alphonse?

RAYMOND: There are special days. I am hoping this week.

KATE: Must be hard. *(Beat)* "Nil". I love this.

RAYMOND: The water?

KATE: It's just— "Nil"? Like "nothing"?

RAYMOND: It is short for "Source du—"

KATE: "Source of the Nile." I know. But all you see is "Nil!" Then look here underneath: "tasted, tested, trusted". It's perfect! "Nothing tasted, nothing tested, nothing trusted!" So, where's the place you want to take me?

RAYMOND: Kibuye. On Lake Kivu, in the West. One of Alan's favorite places. We interviewed some survivors there in the beautiful Catholic church. One of many across Rwanda where people trusted to be safe.

(Gunshots. The PRESIDENTIAL GUARD *crosses with an AK-47, stops to check a list, points to the next house, then runs off. The sounds of soldiers running, tanks and trucks moving up the street. More gunshots)*

(Lights up on THOMAS*)*

THOMAS: I do not dispute the figures. Or that the vast majority of the dead were Tutsi. But no-one died at my hands—I am not a flesh hacker. The word "Genocide" immediately relates our tragedy to the Holocaust, but we have our own history. And Haby? He was no Hitler. In fact, he started out as a moderate, a voice for ethnic tolerance—another irony. But though, he was not, as we say, without charm, he'll go down as an obscure African dictator, a harbinger of genocide. The vicissitudes of history! He needed better P R. And, God forgive me, that was my job.

(THOMAS *pushes his way through a group of people, to the bars of a large pair of locked metal gates. Flood lights.*)

THOMAS: Hey! Hey, Dominique! Hey, over here. Let me in—I need to talk!! *(He holds up two fingers.)*

DOMINIQUE: I am sorry, Thomas. We can only take the French for now. We don't even have enough seats for the ex-pats.

THOMAS: Dominique, it's me. I know this game, okay? You owe me at least one.

DOMINIQUE: Some of them, they are evacuating by car.

THOMAS: One seat. I just need one.

DOMINIQUE: I can't do it, Thomas. Good luck.

THOMAS: Hey, don't you walk away from me! I am an official envoy!!

DOMINIQUE: Were.

THOMAS: Wait. Dominique!

DOMINIQUE: You need to be more practical. It is not up to me. Do as the Americans do. Drive south. Butare then out through Burundi. *(She walks away.)*

THOMAS: You'll regret this, you little shit! I'll find you in Paris. You'll pay for this, you son of a bitch!

RAYMOND: We watch him push back through the crowd to his car. He gets in, then suddenly rolls down the window and vomits.

(FELICIEN, *on his hill.*)

FELICIEN: All my life I am in love. My wife—Beata Mutuze—she died many years ago when Raymond's mother arrived to us. That is the world. Someone is going out as another comes in.
She loved Rwanda, too—these thousand hills; there is power in the red earth. Maybe it is the blood of our ancestors which touches our shoes with every step we

take. That is where Beata lives. I feel her underneath me, take her up by the handful. Once someone visits Rwanda, they are always coming back. There is a magic here, a calling. But in her powerful rivers—the Akagera, the Ruzizi, the Nyabarongo—there is poison now. They need fresh blessings from Imana.

(*Lights come up on* DALLAIRE *in his Kigali UNAMIR office. An old land line telephone is ringing persistently.*)

MARK TWAIN: So whattya think?

DALLAIRE: As if I never left.

MARK TWAIN: I'd venture to say, there's a part of you never did.

DALLAIRE: Why doesn't somebody—

MARK TWAIN: Your office.

DALLAIRE: I can do that?

MARK TWAIN: Your review.

DALLAIRE: Well, I can't just let it—

(DALLAIRE *approaches the desk. A second telephone joins in, then static and broken voices from a radio receiver.*)

MARK TWAIN: Man's bottom impulse is to content a requirement of his nature and training, and thus, acquire peace for his soul.

(DALLAIRE *picks up one of the phones, the lights change.*)

DALLAIRE: (*Talking on #1*) Alo? Yes, I understand, Ma'am, but only two of us here, and calls from all the embassies. No, Ma'am, you are important, but—

(*Ring #2*)

DALLAIRE: Can you hold? (*Picks up #2*) UNAMIR. Hey! Where the hell are you? I need you—we're drowning down here. Everyone's—

(*Ring #3*)

DALLAIRE: *Alo? (Holds on #2/speaks into #1)* Going to have to get back to you, Ma'am—we're working on it. We'll get you out, as soon as we possibly can.

(DALLAIRE *hangs up #1/ring #3*)

DALLAIRE: *Alo?* I've got two calls going with four phones ringing and only two of us manning the—

(Ring #2)

DALLAIRE: Can you hold please?

*(Ring #2/*DALLAIRE *picks up #3)*

DALLAIRE: *Alo?* Helen!? I was getting worried. So glad to hear from you! Can I call you right back? I'm completely—

(Ring #2)

DALLAIRE: You're at home? —What? Where? On the street or the yard? *Alo? Alo?* Yes, I'm right here. Where's Lando? And the kids are with you? But my men are there, yes? Standing guard? Okay, good. Then stay put and stay together. Helen, I'm getting a vehicle over there as soon as— They can't. That's the— Only if fired upon. The fucking mandate. I agree, but—

(Ring #1)

DALLAIRE: Where? On the street?

(The sound of children yelling)

DALLAIRE: How many? How many, Helen? You what?

(Ring #2)

DALLAIRE: Too late for what? Inside the gate? *Alo?* Helen? Helen? Lando?! *Alo?*

(Yelling on the other end of the phone, then several gunshots.)

DALLAIRE: *Alo? Alo? Qu'es qu'il y a?*

(A dial tone. DALLAIRE *slowly hangs up phone #3, and it rings again. He grabs it.)*

DALLAIRE: Alo—Lando?! No, sorry, sir, I was just in the middle of talking to someone else on this same phone and I— Excuse me? I am the officer in charge. I can take down her name, but right now I'm not in a position to— Yessir, I understand you are, sir. But with all due respect, sir, you cannot possibly have the slightest idea what I am presently— I WILL DO THE BEST THAT I CAN, SIR! Washington, sir, is a very long way away at this moment and— Yes sir, I do, I know exactly who you are, but you'll just have to hold!

*(*DALLAIRE *puts down the phone and sees* MARK TWAIN *watching.)*

DALLAIRE: They left us alone.

MARK TWAIN: You had a choice. You chose to stay.

(Ring)

DALLAIRE: Are we finished? Can we go?

MARK TWAIN: Not too much more.

DALLAIRE: I've had it. I'm done.

(Ring)

MARK TWAIN: The call that really mattered.

DALLAIRE: Should have taken more pills. I'm ready to go.

MARK TWAIN: Finish up, sir. Then we're off.

(Ring)

DALLAIRE: Finish up? Finish what?

MARK TWAIN: Might want to pick up, sir. Secretary General's office.

DALLAIRE: *(Picks up)* Alo? This is Dallaire. I see, on his behalf. Of course. I am well aware my Belgian troops

are leaving. Where that puts us? Well, sir, they've
been the backbone of—that's right—best-trained, best-
armed, and most-experienced—that's correct, sir—and
their vehicles. If you'll forgive the expression, sir,
they're the balls of my mission and they're being cut
off. *(Listen)* Well, yes, I think that's fair to say—a lot of
strain here, yes. Only so many times one's calls can be
ignored before a fraying of the patience, of the nerves.
So sir, if you can help me then, to understand, to try
and get this straight—the Secretary General, you say,
wants me to give—That he can only recommend, so I
should give the orders? And he's saying all of them?
Abort the whole damn—yes, sir, now I see. And is he
there with you right now? Could I possibly speak—I
see. Well, forgive me for being blunt, sir, but this is
horseshit. Pure and simple. I hear him talking in the
background. But thank you, you've been very clear
on his behalf. So, let me be as clear as I can, also. We
have thousands of refugees here who are counting on
us. Tens of thousands. To escort them to safety. And
as this is my mission, every goddamn one of them,
sir, is my responsibility. So please, if you would just
turn and tell your boss, say, "Mister Secretary General,
sir, Mister Boutros Boutros-Ghali," tell him, if he does
decide to recommend that course of action, that I—in
no uncertain terms and with all respect—I will not
give that order! Not from me. Tell him, that goddamn
Canadian peacekeeper, Dallaire, refuses to withdraw.

(Lights out. A car door slams offstage. THOMAS *runs in with
a small flashlight.)*

THOMAS: CAT-REEN? CAT-REEN!

*(*THOMAS *picks up a note taped to the television. As he reads
it, there is a knock at the door, and* CAT-REEN *appears, as the
story in her note plays out in front of him. She is wearing
her dress from Paris now, over her slip.)*

CAT-REEN: *Alo?*

MAN'S VOICE: *Alo?* Cat-reen. Let me in.

CAT-REEN: Who are you?

MAN'S VOICE: I am Thomas's friend.

CAT-REEN: He's not here.

MAN'S VOICE: I know. He is a very busy man. Enough for two lives.

CAT-REEN: What do you want? He's coming back soon.

MAN'S VOICE: I want—to meet you. A taste of his life.

CAT-REEN: You are not his friend to be talking like this.

MAN'S VOICE: You should be happy I have not told anyone about you.
Cat-reen!

(MAN *bangs on the door.* THOMAS *protectively leans against it, as he continues to read.*)

CAT-REEN: Go away!

MAN'S VOICE: The world is exciting tonight. Drunken boys roaming the streets like packs of wild dogs, looking for action.

CAT-REEN: Then I will keep the door locked.

MAN'S VOICE: Appetites are big tonight, and I am wanting you to take me in. You will like me, Cat-reen, I promise. Just open the door.

CAT-REEN: I can't. What is your name? I will tell him you were here.

MAN'S VOICE: He's not coming back. He can't be caught here now. I'm your best hope. I will keep you safe. Don't be afraid, Cat-reen. Just open the door. Just take me in.

CAT-REEN: Then you do not know Thomas. He is coming back.

MAN'S VOICE: I was trying to be nice, you stupid bitch. I'll break this fucking door!!

(*As the door jumps,* CAT-REEN *takes the paper from* THOMAS's *hands and writes on it furiously, while watching that the door holds. The banging stops.*)

MAN'S VOICE: You had your chance, *inyenzi* whore! Now you'll see. You'll see who will come!!

(CAT-REEN *listens at the door, then puts the paper back into* THOMAS's *hands and speaks, directly to him, into his eyes.*)

CAT-REEN: Thomas—my dear Thomas, where have you gone? I know you will return for me, but I cannot stay here. I am going to find my mother. There is always sanctuary in her church. We will wait there for you to come. Thomas my darling, come soon!

(CAT-REEN *grabs a few things, checks that it's safe, then runs out the door. Panicked,* THOMAS *starts out, then returns to grab the Polaroid from the table, and runs off.*)

(*In another part of the stage, we hear the sound of Interahamwe whistles and singing. R T L M is heard over a radio.* INNOCENT *appears dressed in the "clown-suit" uniform, dancing at a roadblock.*)

INNOCENT: Now every day is a party, but we work hard. It is not easy to kill so many at a time. But more fun than bending over in the field. What bothers me? No break for lunch. But the R P F is coming, so we must finish the job. And when the whistles tell us the day's work is done, the looting is our reward. Good beer—the Primus—we have as much as we can drink! There is food and radios from their houses! And every day we play music. Music everywhere. Music of freedom. John Lennon, he is understanding us. A celebration of freedom for the Hutu people. 'Imagine!' We finally will be free.

(John Lennon's "Imagine" plays on THOMAS's *car radio, as he rolls down the window of his black government Mercedes, his face lit by firelight from a burning vehicle. A* BELGIAN UNAMIR *soldier, in his blue beret or helmet, approaches.)*

BELGIAN UNAMIR: You can't stop here. Keep moving.

THOMAS: *(Holding up his I D)* I am a Government Envoy—Thomas Sibomana. What happened here?

BELGIAN UNAMIR: Bunch of drunken, uh, guys with clubs and machetes. They forced a Red Cross ambulance off the road, flipped it over.

THOMAS: The driver—is he dead?

BELGIAN UNAMIR: They're all dead. Pulled the patient out, the driver, all of them. This is too fucking much. Too fucking much!

(The crackle of voices on his UNAMIR radio.)

BELGIAN UNAMIR: Repeat? I have an ambulance turned over, everyone dead—over. Say that again—over? Negative—over. How many? Camp Kigali? Some one saw it? Can you confirm—over? *Alo?* Can you confirm—over? What the fuck? *(Raising his rifle and making sure he has a bullet in the chamber.)* Move on. Get away from me!

THOMAS: *(Pulls out the Polaroid)* I am looking for this woman. For my wife. She is my wife.

BELGIAN UNAMIR: Move away, before I finally use this fucking rifle! This place is finished. They killed ten of us tonight! Ten of us! Ten of my friends. It's over!! I hate you fucking niggers!!!! All of you!!!!

*(*THOMAS *guns the engine. The sound of tires squealing, as the lights change.)*

*(*KATE *sits on a bench in a church, reading. She puts it down and sits in silence.* RAYMOND *enters.)*

RAYMOND: They're busy preparing things for tomorrow. They're expecting a lot of people.

KATE: It's almost unbearable. She was a nun?

RAYMOND: Sister Belyse. She saw it all. We have the footage of her, but it's all in Kinyarwanda. This is my own translation.

(RAYMOND *hands it to her.* KATE *reads aloud.*)

KATE: "The concept of Evil existed even before the first sparks of sunlight, before the earth and the sky came together, and before the waters gave birth to the enormous womb of the oceans." —Raymond, this is beautiful.— "Evil existed long before the breath of life, long before the presence of gods on earth. Good was there too, its inseparable brother, its vulnerable alter ego, threatened by time and indifference."

(*A* MAN *enters with a box of photos. He goes to a wire hung across the room and clips photos on it.*)

KATE: How many, did you say?

RAYMOND: Two thousand. They brought their whole families to wait out the trouble. It was their one sure place of sanctuary.

KATE: Should I be here, Raymond?

RAYMOND: You are with us. We did many interviews here. Alan would sit here and the person talking over there.

(KATE *sits where* ALAN *sat, as* RAYMOND *walks over and begins to look at the faces strung on the wire.*)

KATE: "Hatred lies dormant in us all. If tomorrow I saw before me a vast unexplored interior where my previous humiliations, my frustrations could all be avenged? A world in which the laws of a past morality would suddenly vanish and the threat of punishment were removed? Who knows what I might do."

(THOMAS's *face suddenly lights up in another part of the stage by the glare of a big flashlight. He is in his car at a military roadblock. Squinting, he can barely make out the* PRESIDENTIAL GUARD *who has stopped him.)*

PRESIDENTIAL GUARD: I D?

THOMAS: Here.

PRESIDENTIAL GUARD: *(Looking at it)* Sibomana?

THOMAS: *(Pointing to the I D)* Thomas. Yes. I'm with the government.

PRESIDENTIAL GUARD: What party?

THOMAS: M R N D, of course! I'm a senior envoy with Habyarimana. Hutu Power! It's time to finish the job!!

PRESIDENTIAL GUARD: Sibomana? The one from the radio? I know you! We are doing as you tell us—cleaning the streets of *inyenzi* and moderates tonight.

THOMAS: Rwanda for the Hutu!!!

PRESIDENTIAL GUARD: *(Motions him through)* Rwanda for the Hutu! Be careful where you drive tonight, sir. The youth-wingers have their own roadblocks tonight. And they are drinking. Drinking a lot. They are out of control!

(THOMAS *drives on.)*

(*Lights return us to the church, as* KATE *continues to read.)*

KATE: "To erase all humanity. To look no more into the faces of others. To drink enough alcohol to be released from all hesitation, and to wipe out all memory of daily life. To remain in ignorance of doubt so that the act is nothing more than a gesture of unbelievable power. To be master of the slave kneeling at one's feet. God made man."

(KATE *looks over at* RAYMOND *who is sitting now, holding one of the photos from the line. He looks up at her, deeply affected.*)

KATE: Raymond, are you all right?

RAYMOND: 44.

KATE: What?

RAYMOND: (*Indicating the photo*) 44. I found him. I found Felicien.

(*Lights take us back to* THOMAS. *R T L M plays loudly on a portable radio.*)

THOMAS: Rwanda for the Hutu!

(INNOCENT *smacks his panga against* THOMAS's *car roof.*)

INNOCENT: Stop! Wait! Where do you think you are going? This is my roadblock. You must wait like all the others. You must wait.

THOMAS: I am an envoy for Habyarimana—I am a Government Minister.

INNOCENT: You must wait. (*Toking on a joint*)

THOMAS: Here, look at my I D. It is official. I don't have time for this.

INNOCENT: You must make the time. (*To one of his cohorts O S.*) Shut up—I'm looking at his I D. Can you read? CAN YOU READ?! Then shut up!

THOMAS: I am a personal friend of President Habyarimana.

INNOCENT: He is dead now. He has no friends.

THOMAS: Here, this will buy you Primus for the month.

(INNOCENT *looks at him.*)

THOMAS: (*Stuffing more in his hand*) For the year, then. For a lifetime.

INNOCENT: (*Smiles*) You are a friend of Habyarimana?

THOMAS: Was.

INNOCENT: You have shaken his hand?

THOMAS: Of course.

INNOCENT: *(Takes* THOMAS's *hand)* With this same hand?

THOMAS: Yes. Many times.

INNOCENT: This would be a trophy, then, I think. A connection to Rwanda's history. *(He lifts his panga as though to cut it off)*

THOMAS: No, please. Please don't! Don't cut me. Please. I can get you more money.

INNOCENT: *(Lets him go)* Do you like to kill some Tutsi here with us, Mister Minister?

THOMAS: Actually, my—my mother. She's very sick. I need to find her. Get her, I mean.

INNOCENT: *(To the others manning the roadblock)* He needs to get to his mommy. *(He grabs the Polaroid of* CAT-REEN *from the dashboard.)* Who is this? This does not look like Mommy. I could jerk off to a photo like this!

THOMAS: It's my wife. I'm trying to find her.

INNOCENT: Your wife? Very nice. I like her. She looks inyenzi. I would like to fuck her on the hood of your car. We could all fuck her. You could join us, Mr. Minister. Your friend, Kinani, said we must all work together.

(As THOMAS *tries to grab the Polaroid,* INNOCENT *slices his hand with his panga, drawing blood.)*

INNOCENT: Don't worry! I'll find her for you and tell her you miss her—deeply. Now go get your mommy, Mister Minister. Show her what you are like inside. She will be so proud of her Hutu son. Now you are one of us!

(THOMAS *pulls his revolver and trains it on* INNOCENT.)

THOMAS: Give it back.

(INNOCENT *hands back the Polaroid and backs away. As* THOMAS *hits the gas and takes off,* INNOCENT *throws a stone after him, audibly hitting the car as it races away.)*

INNOCENT: *ICYITSO!!!*

(Lights find RAYMOND, *waiting for someone.* ALPHONSE *enters, dressed in the pink, cotton, pajama-style outfits worn by prisoners in Rwanda. He stops, when he sees* RAYMOND, *then continues over to him.)*

ALPHONSE: What are you doing here? This is not visiting day.

RAYMOND: One of the guards—Albert—from soccer.

ALPHONSE: He was not so good.

RAYMOND: He always looked up to you.

ALPHONSE: To me? You were the best player.

RAYMOND: But you—you made him laugh. You know, his brothers they—

ALPHONSE: I heard. His mother, too.

(Pause)

RAYMOND: How do they treat you here?

ALPHONSE: There are too many of us. We must take turns sitting down. But I sing here with the choir.

RAYMOND: Felicien always said you have the voice of an angel.

ALPHONSE: *(Pause)* So, you were in America?

RAYMOND: "The States", they like to say. New York. Then after that, Burundi. Kenya, too. But always returning home. Collecting stories.

ALPHONSE: My mother tells me she has seen you. *(Pause)* So, you are making films?

RAYMOND: Camera and translator. Documentary, Anderson Cooper, C N N. But now I am going to make my own. About Rwanda. I promised Felicien I would return.

ALPHONSE: I remember.

RAYMOND: That I would tell our stories in moving pictures. To people far away. One day, he pointed to the stars and asked if I would show my films out there.

ALPHONSE: What did you tell him?

RAYMOND: I told him, "My dreams are without limits because of you". *(Pause)* You told me you saw him. On his hill. Alive.

ALPHONSE: I did not lie. I saw him.

*(*ALPHONSE *and* RAYMOND *look at each other for a long moment.)*

ALPHONSE: Do you remember Mateus' cousin? Innocent? The one from Burundi? *(He puts his head in his hand for a moment, crosses himself, then looks back up and continues.)* Raymond...I have a story for your camera.

*(*FELICIEN *is sitting on his hill. It is late afternoon.)*

FELICIEN: Rugira! Stay out of there! How many times must I tell you?

*(*ALPHONSE *sets up his story.)*

ALPHONSE: As the R P F got nearer, there was a change. A fourth river appeared. Like no river I have ever seen, it is bigger than all the others. A human river of Hutu. Some who had killed, some not. But all fearing reprisal. Now they became the refugees. Flowing out of the country, away from the R P F. Running for their lives.

(Photos of the exodus are projected, hundreds of thousands of people carrying their belongings, all walking along the road in the same direction.)

ALPHONSE: A flood of human beings flowing endlessly into the Congo, to Zaire. To the base of the reawakened volcano.

(The sound of a number of small pickup trucks is heard down the hill, with men blowing whistles and laughing. FELICIEN looks off towards them.)

(INNOCENT appears over the hill. He has a whistle around his neck, a panga in his belt, and a club studded with nails. In his other hand, he carries two beers at once, which he has clearly been drinking. He is wearing CAT-REEN's dress from Paris. He stops when he sees FELICIEN.)

INNOCENT: Who are you staring at, *Inyenzi*?

FELICIEN: Everyone knows me here. I am Felicien. Felicien Kalisa.

INNOCENT: Are those your cows, cockroach?

FELICIEN: Rugira and Ingizi, yes. They are my family.

INNOCENT: I didn't ask their names.

FELICIEN: Where are you from?

(INNOCENT stares, taking a long drink.)

FELICIEN: Do you have family on this hill? I think I have seen you.

INNOCENT: Did I say you could ask me questions, you old Tutsi snake?

FELICIEN: Oh yes, I remember—you are Mateus' cousin, Innocent! His uncle Bernard is my son-in-law, you know?

INNOCENT: My name is not for you to speak, Inyenzi! I do not want it in your filthy mouth!! I could crush you in a second under my foot!!!

(INNOCENT *approaches* FELICIEN, *then stops and blows
a long, loud blast on his whistle, prompting voices and
whistles from others down the hill. Then he turns and struts
off.*)

RAYMOND: So, you were there?

ALPHONSE: *(Nods)* I saw this happen. I was walking up
the hill.

RAYMOND: And Innocent? What? Did he come back?

ALPHONSE: Innocent was getting high and drinking
beer all afternoon. He and his friends, they had just
come back from a church. In Nyamata. All of them
boasting about what they had done.

RAYMOND: I have seen their work at Nyamata. And
Felicien?

ALPHONSE: *(He takes a breath)* That afternoon—It was
as if the winds blew everyone together. Raymond,
you will not believe—a car, a big black one, suddenly
appears. Leading along the road a grand procession,
such a sight as I have never seen—so many trucks,
rumbling like thunder, coming from the East. And for
some reason, here is where they stop.

(*We hear the sound of a convoy of trucks, insistently
honking their horns as they push through the sea of
humanity, getting nearer. We hear them come to a stop but
continue to idle their engines. The Interahamwe down the
hill offstage give a drunken cheer.*)

(PRESIDENTIAL GUARD *enters.*)

PRESIDENTIAL GUARD: Show your respect. Colonel
Bagasora is coming. Respect!

(PRESIDENTIAL GUARD *fires off three shots. There is
silence.*)

RAYMOND: Bagasora! The Devil himself!

(*COLONEL* BAGASORA *sweeps in, and the* PRESIDENTIAL
GUARD *salutes, as he snaps to attention.* BAGASORA
looks out at the view for a moment, then turns to the
PRESIDENTIAL GUARD.)

BAGASORA: (*To* PRESIDENTIAL GUARD) You'll need those
bullets—the R P F is climbing up our ass! (*He takes swig
from a bottle of Nil water, then addresses the men down the
hill.*) WE MUST FINISH THE JOB. That way there will
be no consequences. But only then. These Tutsi, they
are not Rwandese. They came down from Ethiopia
long ago. We will send them back by the Nyaborongo.
Let their corpses ride the rivers back to where they
came from and leave us our land, our dignity and our
peace! We will be free!! Hutu Power!!!

(*All the Hutus down below join in chanting, "Hutu
Power!!! Hutu Power!!!" and blowing their whistles.*)

BAGASORA: (*Aside to* PRESIDENTIAL GUARD) This is one
of the most beautiful hills in all of Rwanda.

PRESIDENTIAL GUARD: Yes, sir, I agree.

BAGASORA: (*Sniffing the air in the direction of* FELICIEN)
Then for God's sake, take out the trash!

(BAGASORA *sweeps back out the way he came. The*
PRESIDENTIAL GUARD *starts to level his AK-47 at*
FELICIEN, *then thinks better of it. Instead, he blows his
whistle and with an impatient gesture, points* FELICIEN
*out to the Interahamwe below, then hurries off to rejoin the
convoy. We hear the sound of his Mercedes starting up, as
the trucks rev their engines and the whole caravan resumes
their honking, resuming their procession into the West.*)

RAYMOND: Alphonse, those trucks—I know about
them. Full of Rwanda's money—our currency! All of
it!! The genocidaires, they stole it all and ran away.
Escorted by the French. The snake leaving Eden.

ALPHONSE: "What more could happen here?," I asked
myself, but soon I was regretting having even asked
that question. Raymond, I heard a sound I never
will forget. The scream, you know, a kite lets out
descending on its prey? I had never heard this sound
come from a human. Rising up in anger, like a wave
about to crash, Innocent descends upon Rugira.

(A bird's scream)

ALPHONSE: Swooping down, possessed, upon the
unsuspecting bull, he hacks away, cuts deep down
through his spine.

(A bull's bellow)

ALPHONSE: And as Rugira falls, Ingizi tries to run
away,

(Frightened mooing)

ALPHONSE: but Innocent is not to be denied. In one
swift move, he rains his hateful blows upon Ingizi.
Then, rounding with his club, his strength now
doubled by his rage, he breaks her hind legs with a
sickening snap.

(A cow's pained cries)

ALPHONSE: She bellows out in pain and fear, as
Innocent falls further to his task. His eyes bright red,
two setting suns, no longer like a man, he butchers
and desexes them. And poor Ingizi, full of milk, her
mother's sack he bursts and steaming entrails, freed
of walls, unravel on the ground. And still he cuts,
still slashing at their lifeless bodies, cursing with each
blow. 'Til finally, in triumph, though it takes him
many swings, he clears Rugira's head clean from its
home. Then hoisting it above his own, he turns to all
his friends and is rewarded with a deafening warrior's
cheer.

(A loud cheer rises up from his drunken Interahamwe brothers.)

*(*INNOCENT *re-enters, out-of-breath and covered in fresh blood. He carries his bloody panga in one hand, a long, severed horn in the other.)*

INNOCENT: Your children, Inyenzi, they have very bad manners—they refused to share their milk!

(Laughter from INNOCENT'*s friends. He drops the horn in front of* FELICIEN.*)*

INNOCENT: Why do you not teach your children better? Now, get on your knees and apologize for their behavior.

*(*FELICIEN *gets on his knees, as lights shift back to* ALPHONSE *and* RAYMOND.*)*

RAYMOND: I am not sure my stomach is ready for this story.

ALPHONSE: Shall I stop?

RAYMOND: I have to hear it.

ALPHONSE: I know, and I must tell it.

(The lights return us to the scene. INNOCENT *eyes* FELICIEN, *as though amused by the dilemma of where to hit him first.)*

INNOCENT: No wait! We must not waste this chance; a perfect opportunity. Where is the man who hesitates and always strays behind? The farmer. Bring him here! Right now, so he can learn.

*(*INNOCENT *blows his whistle twice, and* ALPHONSE *steps forward uneasily, into the scene.)*

RAYMOND: What is this? Alphonse? What are you doing?

ALPHONSE: I am telling you the truth.

RAYMOND: No, we were like brothers—I have no one left to lose.

(ALPHONSE *takes* INNOCENT's *panga and walks down to where* FELICIEN *kneels.*)

ALPHONSE: You must know, we spoke together—but only with our eyes. As if no-one else existed in that moment.

(*Now we hear that conversation.*)

ALPHONSE: Felicien?

FELICIEN: Alphonse Ngarambe! How is your mother?

ALPHONSE: This cannot be.

FELICIEN: You have Emmanuel's eyes, you know? It's as if I am looking at him!

ALPHONSE: You are too old to be a danger. There is no harm in you.

FELICIEN: Today is my day.

ALPHONSE: This is not possible. I must explain to them...

FELICIEN: Then both of us will die.

ALPHONSE: Are you afraid?

FELICIEN: I am too busy watching. You must remember the story of what happens here today.

ALPHONSE: No, you are the keeper of the stories.

FELICIEN: Are you afraid, Alphonse?

ALPHONSE: Part of me is numb.

FELICIEN: One day you will tell Raymond our story. Of the wave that washed over and carried us away. Alphonse! Do not look away. A man is made up of his choices. Do you understand? If I am to be your first, I must also be your last. You must find the strength to stand against the tide.
I am not the one who will live with this. I am already old.

I have had a good life. "Felicien", you can tell him, "was content".

(INNOCENT *blows his whistle and points to* FELICIEN.)

INNOCENT: Look at the ground, Inyenzi! *(Counselling* ALPHONSE*)* You must never look in their eyes. This is the worst thing you can do. The eyes of someone you kill are immortal. It is a common mistake. You will learn. Just hit him once, then we will finish him off. We are in this together.

RAYMOND: That's enough!

INNOCENT: *(Goes over and marks on* FELICIEN*)* Head cut here. Remember?

RAYMOND: Alphonse!!

INNOCENT: Neck cut to bleed out.

RAYMOND: No—stop! I hate this story!!

INNOCENT: Or hard across the spine. Remember, little brother?

RAYMOND: Alphonse?! Do you hear me?!

INNOCENT: Now, do your work.

(ALPHONSE *steps up behind* FELICIEN.)

RAYMOND: It is a lie! This is not you!!

ALPHONSE: Do you think—

INNOCENT: Time is not our friend in this business. We must finish the job. Or are you icyitso?

ALPHONSE: No!

(*From down the hill, we hear the sounds of truckloads of* INNOCENT's *fellow Interahamwe blowing whistles, slapping machetes against the sides of the trucks, and singing.*)

INNOCENT: You must do this. Do it now! You must not hesitate, farmer boy! The R P F will soon be knocking on our doors. They will rape our wives and eat our children! Do your work and be a man! Do it!! Do it!! Do it—

(FELICIEN *nods his head.* ALPHONSE *takes a deep breath, then brings the machete up over his head.*)

RAYMOND: No, Alphonse!!!

(*Blackout. The sound of a machete cutting through a melon. Lights up on* DALLAIRE, *at a podium, demonstrating with a panga.*)

DALLAIRE: And it happened over. And over. And over. Five times more efficient than the Holocaust. And I could have brought the whole thing to a halt with a few thousand armed troops. The world knew what was happening. They just closed their eyes. I had twenty thousand refugees I was able to move to safety. A drop in the bucket in the face of how many I lost. But twenty thousand human beings. I could not, in good conscience abandon those people. So, I stayed. And was a witness. When what they really needed was a press agent. That was my failure. I couldn't, just couldn't, for the life of me, get the world to care.

(DALLAIRE *steps down to where* MARK TWAIN *waits with his cigar, as* FELICIEN *appears.*)

FELICIEN: One man. One man from far away. He wanted to save us. But his people were not interested. What could he do? In the final days of it all, he passed through our village. A town of only ghosts now. He was so tired, so anguished, so drained of life, it was as if he too was among the dead.
He paused to look down at the latrine, an open grave now filled up with bodies, my family among them— and something caught his eye. Among the twisted limbs and anguished faces, a little boy was moving.

(*The* BOY *enters in his windbreaker and lies down, moving very slightly.*)

KATE: Alan started to tell me about a story from Dallaire's book that affected him, about a boy, but it wouldn't come out.

FELICIEN: Despite the smell of death which stung eyes and throat, he could not leave. He could not walk away from hope.
So, he climbed down. Onto that pile of death. Until he reached the child. Then took him up as if he was his own.

(DALLAIRE *takes the* BOY *up in his arms.* MARK TWAIN *picks up the story.*)

MARK TWAIN: But as he turned to hand him up, he realized the movement he had seen was not of life refusing to give up, but something else entirely. It was maggots. Eating from within. (*To* DALLAIRE) Put him down.

DALLAIRE: I can't.

MARK TWAIN: He's gone. Put him down and move ahead.

(*The sound of a tinny audio system playing martial music*)

DALLAIRE: From the moment I raised the blue and white flag here, it was a sacred trust. I represented the eyes of the world. I gave them my word they'd be safe. I shook their hands and looked in their eyes. The same eyes that still follow me. That will always follow me.

MARK TWAIN: Put him down. Failure's part of finding your way. But it's still up to you. You damn fool, don't you see? You still have choices left. I can only watch.

DALLAIRE: Then close your eyes!

MARK TWAIN: Like everyone else?! The chance to try again, to fight another day—that's all that keeps us alive. Put him down and move ahead.

DALLAIRE: I can't. He's someone's son.

MARK TWAIN: And so are you. Forgiveness, general—

DALLAIRE: What makes my life worth saving?

MARK TWAIN: A man of conscience, General, is a
rare and precious commodity. This battered world
can scarce afford the loss. There's purpose in you.
Goodness.

DALLAIRE: How can you be so sure?

MARK TWAIN: How, sir? How? Well, I think that's
perfectly obvious. Because you picked him up!

FELICIEN: And long he stood there, holding hope
securely in his arms, though clearly none was left.

MARK TWAIN: The god-damned human race.

(RAYMOND *turns on film-style lights, revealing* THOMAS *in
his cell.*)

THOMAS: Of all the ironies, here is my favorite: Right
after the R P F invasion, when I flew to Egypt with
Habyarimana? Haby was in a panic. Completely
spooked. Desperate to buy arms. And we did—six
million dollars worth. Egyptian-made AK-47s, sixty
thousand grenades—paid for through the Commercial
International Bank of Egypt. All carefully disguised,
of course. I'm ashamed to say that was me. Mostly
to prove I wasn't inyenzi. But here's the irony: their
foreign minister, the man who did the deal with us—a
real calculator who spoke in the most graphic detail
about the weapons and drove a hard bargain? Turned
out, he was on his way up in the world. Less than two
years later, he became the sixth Secretary General of
the United Nations—Boutros Boutros-Ghali.
Now, all I have left are memories.
Paulette and I used to take Chantal to the movie
theaters in Paris on the Champs d'Elysee—cushy seats,
red velvet curtains, spiffy women selling candy and
frozen bon-bons—to watch double-features of Clint

Eastwood westerns and stupid French comedies. And
back in Kigali, Cat-reen. The passion. The love. When
I was a boy, we could get to the hills in less than ten
minutes. Goat brochettes by the roadside, spicy with
pilli-pilli sauce. Who knew we'd be Nazis?

(As RAYMOND *turns the film lights off, we hear:)*

V O: Flight 315 now boarding at gate 3. *Le vol 315
embarquement à la porte 3.*

*(*KATE *enters with a carry-on bag.)*

KATE: I was getting worried.

RAYMOND: Sorry. I am here.

KATE: Left you a message. Guy from the memorial
center called me this morning. Something he thought
might appeal to me. A special service, he said, for
unidentified remains.

*(Actors carry on wooden coffins, draped in lace and purple
cloth.)*

KATE: One. After another. After another. Very moving.
Important. That someone be there to see them off. To
say, "You're not alone." To be a part of something
bigger, you know? —of humanity. And then, I look
over and see this white guy standing there, tears
streaming down his face. And I suddenly realize it's
him, it's Dallaire—he's there, too. General Dallaire.
And you know what? He doesn't look like Alan at all.
(A breath) You all right?

RAYMOND: I will miss you.

KATE: I know. Me, too. But, I'm coming back.

RAYMOND: I heard Alphonse…

KATE: Raymond—?

RAYMOND: His mother called to tell me he is being
released.

KATE: Oh. That's— Wow.

RAYMOND: He is coming home.

KATE: How is that for you?

RAYMOND: "Forgiveness is the fragrance that the violet sheds on the heel that has crushed it."

KATE: Do they say that here?

RAYMOND: No, that's Mark Twain. Are you okay to fly?

KATE: Got my music, my book. You know, "if not now—"

RAYMOND: "Come on, Dave—"

KATE: Exactly.

(The exterior scream of airplane engines gradually mutes to interior cabin level. Lights reveal the interior of a commercial airplane. The four front-row seats and a partial view of the next few rows are visible. DALLAIRE enters and sits in the first row by the window. A white male FLIGHT ATTENDANT enters.)

FLIGHT ATTENDANT: Take your jacket, sir?

DALLAIRE: Thank you. Full flight?

FLIGHT ATTENDANT: Couldn't find a manger for Jesus on here today.

DALLAIRE: Glad I made it on.

FLIGHT ATTENDANT: Good to have you with us. Wish I could plop right down next to you, knock a couple back.

KATE: *(To RAYMOND)* For some reason, Alan said, every dream would end with him on an airplane. A big one. And he never knew where it was headed. And it was always full. Everyone was on it. From his past and Dallaire's—boy scouts, college, sometimes his mother and father, who died years ago. Characters from books he'd read. Familiar faces and rows of total strangers.

DALLAIRE: Do you know who those girls are—the ones in the back?

FLIGHT ATTENDANT: School group, I think—a chorus. I'll see if we can get 'em to serenade us later. Let me know if you need anything.

(*The* FLIGHT ATTENDANT *heads back to attend to other passengers.* KATE *sits in the opposite first row window seat from* DALLAIRE, *pulls out an ipod, and looks out the window. The* FLIGHT ATTENDANT *re-enters, trips, and drops something.*)

DALLAIRE: Are you all right?

FLIGHT ATTENDANT: Yeah, just zero sleep this week— friend in the hospital.

DALLAIRE: Oh, I'm sorry.

FLIGHT ATTENDANT: Not your fault! Okay now— energy, service face—gotta get to work. Start you off with a little champagne?

DALLAIRE: Just water.

FLIGHT ATTENDANT: Coming right up.

KATE: Could I maybe get a mimosa? Thanks.

(*The* FLIGHT ATTENDANT *exits.*)

(*On* FELICIEN's *hill, light reveals a familiar silhouette with his hat and staff. But as he stands, we see it is* RAYMOND, *holding his camera. Projected large, we see what* RAYMOND's *camera sees; rivers, hills, and lush vegetation—a stunning view.*)

(*On the plane, a large man enters, his back to us. The* FLIGHT ATTENDANT *returns with* DALLAIRE's *water.*)

FLIGHT ATTENDANT: Take your jacket, sir?

(*The man mumbles something.*)

FLIGHT ATTENDANT: I'm sorry?

(The man mumbles again and turns. It is BAGASORA. DALLAIRE *turns immediately away.)*

FLIGHT ATTENDANT: Well, let me see what we've got. Not sure we have Crown Royal.

*(*DALLAIRE *motions to* FLIGHT ATTENDANT.*)*

FLIGHT ATTENDANT: *(To* DALLAIRE*)* Change your mind about that drink?

DALLAIRE: I left something in my jacket.

FLIGHT ATTENDANT: No problem.

*(*FLIGHT ATTENDANT *brings his jacket,* DALLAIRE *pulls out a prescription bottle, then hands it jacket back.)*

DALLAIRE: Thank you—I'm sorry, what is your name?

FLIGHT ATTENDANT: I'm Larry.

DALLAIRE: Thank you, Larry.

*(*FLIGHT ATTENDANT *heads up the row, doing final inspections.)*

FLIGHT ATTENDANT: Ma'am, seat forward for take-off— you know the drill!

*(*MELVIN PHILLIPS, *a black American businessman rushes in and sits in the empty seat next to* KATE, *who continues to look out the window, listening to music.)*

PHILLIPS: *(Across the aisle to* DALLAIRE*)* That was close— couldn't get off the phone.

*(*PHILLIPS's *Blackberry rings.)*

PHILLIPS: Oh shit. *(Takes it)* Warren? Gotta call you back, dude, we're about to take off. I'm on it—I'll send those files.
Later. *(Hangs up and puts it away)* Everyone's all excited.

DALLAIRE: Excited?

PHILLIPS: I mean, it's sad, you know, but the
devastation this country suffered left a void in which—
the infrastructure here is nonexistent—you can start
from scratch: state-of-the-art phone system, power
grid, architecture, anything—oh my god, banking!

FLIGHT ATTENDANT: *(In the back)* Um, sir, I hope
you're not intending to light that in here, are ya? Non-
smoking flight. Hello? Welcome to the 21st Century—
they're all non-smoking flights!

DALLAIRE: Banking?

PHILLIPS: I do viability assessment for foreign
investment, okay? And let me tell you, Rwanda's could
become to Africa what Singapore is to Asia; a central
banking hub—a place you can trust absolutely—it's
fucking huge! And the methane gas they're finding in
Lake Kivu?

DALLAIRE: I know there's a smell there, but…

PHILLIPS: You know why? Because every thousand
years, all this vegetation pours into the lake, releasing
huge amounts of carbon monoxide. And it's all primed
for another one right now! A fuel reserve so large, they
could power to burn and still have plenty for export!
We're talking a complete overhaul of the economy—a
massive boost. Rwanda is on the path to becoming the
jewel of central Africa. I'm Melvin Phillips, by the way.

DALLAIRE: I'm—

PHILLIPS: No need, sir—I know exactly who you are,
and it's an honor! A total honor. Let me give you my
card. You know, we could use a real-life hero on our
board. Wouldn't have to do anything. All just about
credibility, you know? Think about it. You've got my
number. Now if you'll excuse me—been running from
one meeting to another since I got here.

(PHILLIPS *pops a sleeping pill, puts on his sleep mask and neck pillow, turns off his overhead light and is out.*)

(DALLAIRE *downs a pill with his water, sneaks a look at* BAGASORA, *then takes another.* FLIGHT ATTENDANT *returns.*)

DALLAIRE: Um, excuse me—Larry? Think I will, after all.

FLIGHT ATTENDANT: Decided to celebrate a little, did you? (*Indicating empty seat*) Guess this guy's not gonna make it, after all. This is your lucky day! But I may have to get you that drink once we're up in the air cause—Oh, wait. (*Reaching into his apron*) Well, look at me!

FLIGHT ATTENDANT: Still packing these cute little vials from the last flight. Looks like Uncle Larry's got your poison right here.

(FLIGHT ATTENDANT *slips* DALLAIRE *a couple of small bottles his apron pocket, then moves away.* KATE *speaks to* DALLAIRE.)

KATE: Excuse me…

DALLAIRE: Sorry? (*For the first time, he looks at* KATE.)

KATE: Are you—Are you all right?

DALLAIRE: I'm—Yes, I'm fine. Thanks. You?

KATE: Me too. I am. All right.

(MARK TWAIN's *voice is heard over the P A.*)

MARK TWAIN: (*V O*) Flight attendants prepare for departure.

FLIGHT ATTENDANT: Okay, let's get this turkey up in the air.

DALLAIRE: No, wait. I shouldn't have these. (*Hands the bottles back*) I'm on medication. I can't.

FLIGHT ATTENDANT: Glad you remembered. Don't want you leavin' this plane on a stretcher.

DALLAIRE: No. That would have been a mistake.

FLIGHT ATTENDANT: All right then, fasten your seatbelts 'cause here we go!

(Static and a ding, and again we hear MARK TWAIN's voice.)

MARK TWAIN: *(V O) Allons-y!*

(The lights in the cabin go out, and we hear the sound of the airplane taking off. Then, the chorus of young African girls is heard singing in the back of the plane. FELICIEN appears behind a scrim, as though he is suspended in mid-air.)

FELICIEN: There is a story that has become famous in Rwanda about a group of schoolgirls.

(RAYMOND's camera tells the same story in pictures—faces of schoolgirls, smiling and laughing together.)

FELICIEN: Their teachers had been instructed to separate the students into Hutu and Tutsi. They all knew, of course. They knew each other intimately. And they all had I D cards to remind them.

(We see the schoolhouse from a distance, and gradually move towards it.)

FELICIEN: When the Militia showed up at the classroom door with machetes and clubs and ordered the Tutsi out, the girls refused. They took hands and stood together. "We are not Hutu and Tutsi", they said. "We are Rwandan. We are friends." All that were there were killed. Every single one. After another. After another.

(The doors open, revealing a bare, room with dark stains on the walls and clothing draped over two crossing ropes in the center.)

FELICIEN: Sometimes language fails me. Is there a word for when you have violated your own existence so thoroughly that your identity disappears into a well of sorrow, leaving only broken traces of what it once meant to be human? What do we call that?

(Projected, we see a gallery of Rwandese faces.)

(Lights return us to the cabin, where asleep in the seat next to DALLAIRE, *we see the* BOY. DALLAIRE *gently puts a blanket over him, and the scene recedes back into darkness.)*

(The camera ascends into the air, flying over beautiful rivers, hills and valleys, over forests and the famous mountain gorillas…)

FELICIEN: And how do you even begin to describe a genocide?

(…then over Lake Kivu, the ocean…)

FELICIEN: It is like trying to describe the sea to someone who has never seen it by showing them a handful of water.

(…and out into space.)

(Thunder. The sound of heavy rain. We see CAT-REEN, *dressed only in her slip, covered with blood and dirt, lying motionless, face-up on the ground.* RAYMOND *approaches with his camera, her face projected large across the theater.)*

FELICIEN: It is important to remember that it was not eight hundred thousand, or a million, people that were killed.

*(*CAT-REEN's *eyes blink open.)*

FELICIEN: It was one person. Then another. Then another. Every face. Every life. Every story.

(Slowly, CAT-REEN *sits up, gets to her feet, and begins to walk, one careful step at a time.* RAYMOND *follows her with his camera, until he sees* ALPHONSE *enter in civilian clothes.*

RAYMOND *puts down the camera, and the two friends stand looking at each other.)*

(FELICIEN *appears above them, sitting on the airplane wing. Next to him, the figure of another man. In a white suit, smoking a cigar. The smoke curls up into the light, which slowly fades…to black.)*

END OF PLAY